More than any other American, John C. Calhoun is associated with the theory of *states' rights*. As one of the most important Southern senators in the decades before the Civil War, Calhoun's speeches and writings found wide national support. In advocating *state sovereignty* above *national union,* this fiery man did what his conscience bade him.

This penetrating analysis of Calhoun's life and thought seeks to appraise the role his theories played in the tragic Civil War that split a nation asunder. It is also an important document in the history of the *states' rights* question, still a burning national controversy.

him to universities in Japan, India, Europe, and South America. During 1962-63 Professor Current was on leave from Wisconsin as Harmsworth Professor at Oxford University.

On the Board of Editors for the *American Historical Review* since 1960, Professor Current has been kept busy with activities connected with various hist

He has written (

ing articles for

and the *Encyclo*

Among his book

ures is *Lincoln the President: Last Full Measure,* written with J. G. Randall, which won the Bancroft Prize for History in 1956.

THE
GREAT
AMERICAN
THINKERS
SERIES

This new series of original works is designed to present in highly readable form the flow of American thought from colonial times to the present. Each volume has been written by a leading scholar and is devoted to a single man in the history of American thought who represents a particular trend or movement within the great span of our culture. Each book in the series contains a short biography of the man, a critical evaluation of his central ideas and their influence upon American thought as a whole, as well as an extensive bibliography and an index.

The Great American Thinkers Series is designed for the general reader as well as the serious college student or higher-level secondary school student, and is under the general editorship of two distinguished American educators: Thomas S. Knight, Ph.D., Associate Professor of Philosophy, Utica College of Syracuse University; and Arthur W. Brown, Ph.D., Professor of English and former Chairman of the Division of Languages, Utica College of Syracuse University. JOHN C. CALHOUN was written by Richard N. Current, Ph.D., Professor of History, University of Wisconsin.

THE GREAT AMERICAN THINKERS SERIES

The first twelve volumes in the series will be:

THOMAS JEFFERSON, by Stuart Gerry Brown, Ph.D., Maxwell Professor of American Civilization, Syracuse University.

JOHN C. CALHOUN, by Richard M. Current, Ph.D., Professor of History, University of Wisconsin.

CHAUNCEY WRIGHT, by Edward Madden, Ph.D., Professor of Philosophy, San Jose State College.

In preparation:

CHARLES PEIRCE, by Thomas S. Knight, Ph.D., Associate Professor of Philosophy, Utica College of Syracuse University.

THEODORE PARKER, by Arthur W. Brown, Ph.D., Director of the Institute of Humanities and Chairman of the English Department, Adelphi University.

WILLIAM JAMES, by Edward C. Moore, Ph.D., Graduate Dean and Coordinator of Research, University of Massachusetts.

JOHN WOOLMAN, by Edwin H. Cady, Ph.D., Rudy Professor of English, University of Indiana.

GEORGE BANCROFT, by Russel B. Nye, Ph.D., Professor of English, Michigan State University.

THORSTEIN VEBLEN, by Douglas Down, Ph.D., Associate Professor of Economics, Cornell University.

BENJAMIN FRANKLIN, by Ralph L. Ketcham, Ph.D., Associate Editor of the *Papers of Benjamin Franklin*, Yale University, and Professor of American Studies, Syracuse University.

JONATHAN EDWARDS, by Alfred Owen Aldridge, Ph.D., Professor of English and Director of the Program of Comparative Literature, University of Maryland.

JOHN DEWEY, by Richard J. Bernstein, Ph.D., Associate Professor of Philosophy, Yale University, and Assistant Editor of *Review of Metaphysics*.

JOHN C. CALHOUN

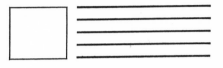

Author of this volume: Richard N. Current, Ph.D., Professor of History, University of Wisconsin.

Series Editors: Thomas S. Knight, Ph.D., Associate Professor of Philosophy, Utica College of Syracuse University; and Arthur W. Brown, Ph.D., Professor of English and former Chairman of the Division of Languages, Utica College of Syracuse University.

Twayne Publishers, Inc.   ::   New York

This Twayne Publishers edition
is published by special arrangement with
Washington Square Press, Inc.

TABLE OF CONTENTS

Chronology   vii

Part 1. The Man and His Career   3

    Family Background and Education   4

    The Nationalist   6

    The Nullificationist   13

    The Sectionalist and Slavery Advocate   19

Part 2. The Theory of Government   37

    State-Rights Precedents   37

    Assumptions: Government and Man   43

    The Concurrent Majority   49

    Nullification   60

    State Powers and Slavery   76

    The Class Struggle   86

    Summary   102

Part 3. Significance and Influence   109

    The Uses of Logic   112
    Conservative and Reactionary: Webster and Calhoun   119

    From Jefferson to Jefferson Davis   127

    The Neo-Calhounism of the Twentieth Century   136

    The Continuing Relevance   148

[v]

Part 4. Literature of the Subject   155

       Calhoun's Own Writings   155

       Biographies   157

       Some Studies of Political Thought   158

       Views of the Neo-Calhounites   160

       Dissenting Views   162

Notes   165

Index   177

John C. Calhoun
Chronology

1782—Born (March 18) near Abbeville, in Ninety-Six District, South Carolina.

1802—Enters Yale College as a junior.

1804—Graduates from Yale (September 12).

1805—Enters the Litchfield, Connecticut, law school, to remain there for about a year and a half.

1807—Begins law practice in Abbeville. Elected (October 13) to the South Carolina general assembly, where he is to serve for two years.

1810—Elected (October) for the first of his three successive terms as a South Carolina representative in Congress.

1811—Marries Floride Calhoun (January 8) and begins his congressional career (November 4).

1812—Introduces bill for war against Great Britain (June 3).

1816—Sponsors incorporation of the second Bank of the United States, supports the bill for a protective tariff, and proposes federal expenditures for internal improvements.

1817—Accepts appointment, which he is to hold for eight years, as Secretary of War in the Monroe Administration.

1821—Declares himself a presidential candidate.

1824—Elected Vice-President of the United States.

1825—Inaugurated (March 4) as Vice-President. Adopts as his permanent residence the Fort Hill plantation in South Carolina.

1827—Defeats the Woolens Bill, for raising tariffs, by casting his vote in the Senate to break a tie.

1828—Writes "The South Carolina Exposition," which the legislature publishes without his name. Re-elected Vice-President.

1831—Quarrels with President Jackson.

1832—Assists in the adoption of the Nullification Ordinance (November 24). Resigns the Vice-Presidency (December 28) after election to the United States Senate.

1833—Defends nullification in debate with Webster. Co-operates with Clay in the passage of the compromise tariff.

1834—Joins with Webster and Clay in opposition to Jackson's bank policy but asserts independence from both major parties.

1836—Condemns abolitionist publications and claims for his state the right to exclude them from the mails.

1837—Defends slavery as a "positive good." Begins to cooperate with President Van Buren and the Democrats.

1841—Leads the fight against the Whig program in Congress. Begins to seek the Democratic nomination for the presidency.

1843—Withdraws from the Senate, after ten years there, to concentrate on his presidential aspirations. Begins to write his *Disquisition on Government* and his *Discourse on the Constitution and Government of the United States*.

1844—Quits the presidential contest (January 20). Appointed Secretary of State by President Tyler. Negotiates Texas annexation treaty, which fails to get Senate approval.

1845—Again elected to the Senate. Presides over the Memphis Railroad Convention.

1846—Opposes going to war with Mexico.

1847—Calls for Southern unity in opposition to the Wilmot Proviso.

1848—Insists upon the organization of Oregon as a territory open to slavery.

1849—Invites Southern congressmen to a conference and prepares an address to the Southern people. Completes his *Disquisition* and most of his *Discourse*.

1850—Denounces compromise in his last great speech (March 4) and in his final remarks (March 13). Dies in Washington (March 31).

Part 1

THE MAN AND HIS CAREER

"Judged by later times and his meaning for them, Calhoun stands in the first rank of men America has produced," one of his biographers concluded a hundred years after his death. "For as a thinker and prophet he was more important for later times than his own." [1]

A number of present-day Americans share this view of John C. Calhoun. They consider him as somehow more relevant to the twentieth century than any of his political contemporaries, including his great rivals Daniel Webster and Henry Clay. His admirers look upon him as a defender of minority rights and an inventor of democratic techniques.

If the neo-Calhounites are to be believed—if Calhoun speaks for the democratic-minded citizens or for the minorities of today—then he is, indeed, more important for our times than for his. Not only that. He must also have a rather different significance now than a century and more ago.

To understand fully the meaning of his ideas for his own time, if not also for ours, we must review the circumstances in which Calhoun presented them. He wrote and spoke as a politician and advocate, not as a disinterested scholar or philosopher, though there was much of the scholar and the philosopher in him. He put forth his thoughts in the course of a long political career, extending from 1810, when he first ran for Congress, to 1850, when he died. During those forty years he served, at one time or another, as Congressman, Secretary of War, Vice-President, Secretary of State, and United States Senator. And he aspired continually to become President.

For approximately the first third of his career he was a nationalist who urged the bold use of governmental powers to develop and strengthen the country as a whole. For the remaining two-thirds, he was a state-rights man and a sectionalist who strove to limit the powers of the federal government and thus to protect the interests of the South, that is, the interests of the slaveowners.

FAMILY BACKGROUND AND EDUCATION

Slavery and state rights featured the world that Calhoun first knew, in the back country of South Carolina, where he was born on March 18, 1782. He was descended from Scotch-Irish pioneers who, in these Carolina hills, had faced the danger of hostile Indians (one of his grandmothers had died in a massacre) and then, during the Revolutionary War, had faced the danger of British redcoats and American Tories. His father, Patrick Calhoun, prospered after the war. By 1790, when John was eight years old and the first federal census was taken, his father owned thirty-one slaves, a larger number than most slaveholders owned in his part of the state. Patrick Calhoun also rose to prominence in local affairs. He opposed the ratification of the United States Constitution in 1787–88. Already he had fought a war on account of taxation without representation, and he feared that the new Constitution would revive the very same evil, for it would permit the representatives of other states to impose taxes upon the people of South Carolina.

When his father died, John was fourteen and was studying at a log-cabin academy operated by his brother-in-law, Moses Waddell. He now left school, worked on the family farm for a few years, and then decided to resume his studies and go on to college. With the financial support of his brothers, he went back to Waddell's academy for a while. At twenty, he left for faraway Connecticut, to enroll as a junior at Yale.

In those days Yale was the intellectual home of the extreme New England Federalists who, now that Thomas Jefferson was President, turned his state-rights arguments against him in opposing almost everything he did or tried to do. The college president, Timothy Dwight, was fond of denouncing the Jeffersonians as atheists and Jacobin revolutionaries. After two years in this intellectual atmosphere, during which he won election to Phi Beta Kappa, Calhoun was graduated. For commencement he prepared an address on "the qualifications necessary to constitute a perfect statesman." After leaving Yale, he spent a year in Litchfield, Connecticut, at the law school of Judge Tapping Reeve, another state-rights Federalist.

Upon the completion of his studies, at twenty-four, Calhoun was a tall, wiry, handsome man, with black hair and burning eyes. Like the devout Calvinist he was, he took life seriously and had little time or inclination for fun. He lacked a sense of humor. He also lacked money and social position, but he possessed plenty of self-confidence, ambition, and determination. The wealth and position that he wanted, he was in due time to get by marriage.

While a student in New Haven and in Litchfield, he had occasionally visited and often corresponded with Mrs. Floride Calhoun, a South Carolina low-country aristocrat, his cousin's widow and heir, who summered at Newport, Rhode Island. Mrs. Calhoun had a daughter, also named Floride, who was ten years younger than Calhoun. Through the mother, he began to court the daughter. Eventually he got permission to woo the young Floride directly, by mail. He is said to have composed and sent her a love poem each line of which began with "Whereas" except the last line, which began with "Therefore." In 1811, when he was approaching twenty-nine, the two were married in the bride's home near Charleston.

Before the year's end, without waiting for the birth of his first child, Calhoun left his bride to go to Washington and sit with Congress. From that time on, his career always took precedence over his family life.[2]

THE NATIONALIST

During the session of 1811–12 Congress wrestled with the problem of the proper American response to current British policy. The British impressed seamen from American ships, infringed upon neutral rights, and abetted the Indians who threatened the Northwestern frontier. The new young congressmen from the frontier areas, Jeffersonian Republicans who followed the lead of Henry Clay, of Kentucky, demanded the use of force. They were dubbed War Hawks, and Calhoun was one of them. Clay put him on the Foreign Affairs Committee. As acting chairman and then chairman of this key committee, Calhoun took an important part in preparing Congress and the people for war. He called for patriotism. "The honor of a nation is its life," he said. "Deliberately to abandon it, is to commit an act of political suicide." [3] He introduced the resolution for declaring war on Great Britain.

Throughout the War of 1812 Calhoun contended, against the obstructionism of New England state-rights men like Daniel Webster, of New Hampshire, for measures and men with which to win the war. He came to be hailed as "the young Hercules who carried the war on his shoulders."

After the return of peace, Calhoun rose to be majority leader of the Jeffersonian Republicans in the House. He used his influence to promote what he referred to as an "enlarged policy" and what Clay called the American System. This was a program of national planning for prosperity and defense. According to the program, the federal government was to levy tariffs for protecting and encouraging manufactures, set up a bank for providing a uniform currency and abundant credit, and spend freely to build a network of highways and waterways. Calhoun was especially enthusiastic about transportation improvements (then commonly known as "internal improvements"). "We are under the most imperious obligation to counteract every tendency to disunion," he declared. "Let us, then, bind the republic together with a perfect system of roads and canals. Let us conquer space." [4]

Clay and Calhoun succeeded in two of the three items in their postwar legislative program. Congress passed and President James Madison signed a bill imposing protective duties (the Tariff of 1816) and another establishing a second Bank of the United States. Congress also passed—but the President vetoed—a bill for devoting to internal improvements the "bonus" and the annual sums which the bank was to pay for its charter. Though Madison professed to favor the betterment of transportation, he thought he saw in the Constitution serious impediments to federal expenditure for that purpose.

Calhoun was disgusted by Madison's constitutional reasoning. "I am no advocate for refined arguments on the Constitution," he said. "The instrument was not intended as a thesis for the logician to exercise his ingenuity on. It ought to be construed with plain, good sense; and what can be more express than the

Constitution on this very point?" [5] Nothing, obviously, could be more explicit than the constitutional authority for spending on the improvement of transportation, for the Constitution in so many words gave Congress the power to lay taxes and provide for the common defense and the general welfare. So it seemed to Calhoun in 1817—about a decade before he himself began, as a logician, to exercise his ingenuity upon the Constitution.

That same year he received his first appointment to an administrative position, as Secretary of War in the cabinet of James Monroe. Immediately the new Secretary undertook to bring vigor and system into the affairs of his department. In his plans for extensive border and coastal fortifications he was frustrated by the parsimony of Congress and the Treasury, but he carried forward the work of removing the Indian tribes to the West, and he provided for regulating the Indian trade through the licensing of private traders and the competition of government trading posts. He also reorganized the army supply services, unified and clarified the command system, reinvigorated the academy at West Point, and cut the cost-per-man of maintaining the armed forces. In his eight years in office he gained, as he deserved, a lasting reputation as one of the ablest of War Secretaries—one to be compared, in later generations, with such successors as Jefferson Davis, Elihu Root, and Henry L. Stimson.

While Calhoun was in the War office, there occurred three events that were vitally to affect his future, though at that time he could not be fully aware of their significance. First, in 1817, General Andrew Jackson led his army on a punitive raid into Florida, then Spanish territory, and Secretary Calhoun, as Jackson's superior, sought in vain to have him reprimanded. Second, the Panic of 1819 touched off a business depression that aroused popular discontent and thus heightened political and sectional tensions. Third, the Missouri controversy of 1819–21, when Northern politicians tried to prevent the admission of Missouri as a slave state, awakened Jefferson like "a fire-bell in the night" and increased the sectionalization of politics—which, in turn, destroyed Calhoun's chances of riding into the presidency, at an early date, on a wave of nationalism such as he had been seeking to arouse.

The omens were not immediately clear. In 1821, at thirty-nine, Calhoun thought he saw a presidential opportunity by 1824. Other members of Monroe's cabinet were in the running; why not he? There was John Quincy Adams, of Massachusetts, the Secretary of State, and there was William H. Crawford, of Georgia, the Secretary of the Treasury. There was also Clay, the Speaker of the House. Calhoun felt he was as good a man and had as good a chance as any of the three. No opposition was to be expected from the Federalist party, for it was now defunct as a national organization. All the contenders belonged to the Republican party.

Before long Calhoun's calculations were upset by an outsider: by General Jackson, the hero of New Orleans, who had the backing of astute politicians in his home state of Tennessee and in other states. Calhoun counted upon the votes of Pennsylvania, for the Pennsylvanians were devout protectionists and so was he, as his record in Congress demonstrated. Yet, long before election time, the Pennsylvanians clearly showed their preference for Jackson. Reluctantly but wisely Calhoun withdrew from the presidential campaign and entered the vice-presidential. He doubled his chances of success by running on two tickets, with both Jackson and Adams.

In 1824 no candidate gained a majority of the electoral vote, so the final choice was left to the House of Representatives. Clay threw his support to Adams, and the House chose him as President. Then Adams, once he had been inaugurated, appointed Clay as Secretary of State. It appeared that Adams, in return for Clay's assistance, was naming Clay as his successor, for most of the previous Secretaries of State, like Adams himself, had succeeded to the presidency. Raising the cry of "corrupt bargain," the Jacksonians began at once to campaign for vindicating Jackson—the people's choice, they said—at the very next election. Calhoun, while Adams' Vice-President, cooperated with the Jacksonians to bring about Adams' defeat in 1828. That year he ran again for the vice-presidency, but on the Jackson ticket only.

Meanwhile Calhoun and other political leaders throughout the nation had been brought to reconsider their views on national policy in consequence of economic changes that were affecting the various regions in different ways. Earlier, as a congressman, he had been free to urge nationalistic policies because his own constituents in South Carolina, or large numbers of them, had favored such policies. As late as 1816 a majority of the South Carolina representatives in Congress had voted for the protective tariff. At that time it seemed that the state had a promising future in industrialization, for she possessed ample water power which might be used for manufacturing textiles in the same areas where the cotton itself was grown.

After 1816, however, the Carolinians devoted themselves more and more to planting, and few mills appeared. The planters came to look upon the tariff as no help but a hurt to them. It cut down imports and hence exports. By reducing the foreign market for cotton, it lowered the price of what the planters sold; by limiting the competition of foreign with domestic manufactures, it raised the cost of what they had to buy. It produced revenues with which to pay for internal improvements, and these in turn were cited in justification of the tariff. Most of the internal improvements, the Carolinians and other Southerners felt, provided connections between the Northeast and the Northwest and thus encouraged the growth of the North at the expense of the South.

While Southerners were turning against the tariff (and internal improvements as well), New Englanders were coming to its support. Among New Englanders, as among Southerners, ideas changed with changing interests. A majority of New England representatives, including Daniel Webster, had voted against the Tariff of 1816, because the predominant interest of their region then lay in the shipping business, in the import trade. But Jefferson's Embargo and the War of 1812 stimulated the rise of cotton mills along the streams of New England. Merchants and shipowners put more and more of their accumulated profits into manufacturing. By about 1830 New England sentiment was to be, on balance, protectionist. By then Webster, once a free trader, already was a tariff advocate, and he was to devote the rest of his career to refuting his own early arguments.

The middle states, especially Pennsylvania, had been protectionist all along. Their representatives, together with allies from other sections, obtained an increase in duties in 1824. In 1827 the Woolens Bill would have raised still higher the rates on manufactured wool. The bill passed the House but was held up by a tie vote in the Senate. As the Senate's presiding officer, Calhoun could cast the deciding vote. He now made a choice that marked the beginning of the end of his nationalist phase. He voted no.

The defeat of the Woolens Bill aroused protectionists everywhere to renewed efforts, and these culminated, in 1828, in an act imposing the highest general level of duties yet. The Tariff of 1828 resulted from a good deal of logrolling, the motives for which were mixed.

John Randolph of Roanoke said the measure was concerned with no manufactures except the manufacture of a President, and there was a bit of truth in his remark. Certainly some of the Congressmen who tacked on amendments did so in the hope of unmaking Adams as President and making Jackson President instead. The scheme was to produce a bill so outrageous that Adams would have to veto it and thus would lose protectionist votes in the fall. Other congressmen, however, sincerely desired protection for this or that commodity—for the cotton products and the wool and woolens of New England, the hemp of Kentucky, the lead of Missouri, even the lemons of Florida. Webster now made *his* great reversal and, though protesting some of the bill's features, cast his vote for the measure as a whole. It passed, and President Adams signed it.

Southerners dubbed the new law the Tariff of Abominations and, particularly in South Carolina, blamed all their economic troubles on it. The troubles of South Carolina were real enough. Plantation profits were declining, abandoned fields were filling with sedge grass, roads and bridges were falling into disrepair, and people were leaving the state in such numbers as to check its population growth. For all this the tariff was blamed. Certainly it did not help, but in fact there were other and more important causes. On the red clay of Carolina, eroded and relatively worn out, cotton growers could not compete with those on the fresher and richer lands of the Black Belt or the farther Southwest.

In South Carolina a faction of radicals demanded immediate and drastic action. They talked of withdrawing their state from the Union that treated them so ill. They would escape the tariff levies through secession. They advocated revolution, no less. And they were rapidly becoming a majority in the state.

Calhoun had to keep the state's support if he was to remain in politics. He needed Jackson's friendship and Northern backing if he was to succeed Jackson as President. He could not do this if he joined the Carolina revolutionaries. He could do still less if he defied them.

THE NULLIFICATIONIST

Thus, in 1828, Calhoun confronted a dilemma. That summer, in the quiet of his Carolina plantation, he tried to work his way out of it. He had to satisfy the Secessionists in his state without antagonizing the Unionists throughout the country. To do so, he had to find a *legal* and *constitutional* alternative to the revolutionary program of secession. He discovered or thought he discovered such an alternative in the theory of nullification which, before the summer's end, he developed and wrote down. Later that year, though neither endorsing his ideas nor naming him as their author, the state legislature published them in a pamphlet entitled "The South Carolina Exposition."

In "The South Carolina Exposition" he argued, with persuasive logic, to three main conclusions. First, the protective tariff was both unfair and unconstitutional. Second, the people of a state, being sovereign, had the right to nullify an unconstitutional law, such as the tariff; and the law would then be null and void in that state until the Constitution should be amended so as to give Congress the power in dispute; when and if this happened the aggrieved state could still secede as a last resort. Third, for the present the people of South Carolina should postpone the exercise of their right, so as to allow Congress an opportunity to rectify its constitutional error and relieve the suffering planters.[6]

[13]

Calhoun had good reasons for being cautious and remaining anonymous, as he did in 1828 and for three years afterward. In 1828, while he was running for Vice-President on the Jackson ticket, nullification might well have been an embarrassment to him and his party. He hoped that Jackson, once he was in the White House, would use his tremendous influence to bring about a drastic reduction of the tariff. Thus the South Carolina Radicals, whom the nullification argument had persuaded to wait, would be finally appeased. And thus Calhoun, his fame untouched by state-rights heresy, would be eligible to go on to the presidency after a term or two for Jackson.

The Jackson-Calhoun ticket won the election of 1828, all right, but nothing else went the way Calhoun had hoped. He soon had to fend against a most resourceful rival for Jackson's favor, Martin Van Buren, the Little Magician of New York. Van Buren obtained the office of Secretary of State for himself and other choice political jobs for his friends. He made use of the Eaton affair further to ingratiate himself with, and estrange Calhoun from, the President. Peggy O'Neal Timberlake Eaton, the wife of Jackson's War Secretary, met snubs from the other cabinet wives, who considered her a loose woman and, even worse, a social climber. The gallant Jackson defended her virtue and insisted that all his followers accept her presence. Van Buren, a widower, ostentatiously did so. Calhoun, then living with his wife and mother-in-law in the latter's Georgetown mansion, could not well do the same, for his womenfolk were among those most shocked by Mrs. Eaton's pretensions. The President finally broke with the Vice-President when he received documentary proof that Calhoun, as Monroe's Secretary of War in 1817, had tried to censure Jackson on account of the Florida raid.

The two men differed on doctrinal as well as personal grounds. In the Webster-Hayne debate (January, 1830), Robert Y. Hayne of South Carolina presented the nullification doctrine on the floor of the Senate, while Calhoun in the presiding officer's chair nodded in approval. At a Jefferson Day dinner soon afterward, Calhoun along with other party notables waited for Jackson's toast, to see whether Jackson sympathized with the state-rights view. The President now made his position clear: "Our Federal Union! It *must* and *shall be* preserved!" When Calhoun's turn came he could only counter with: "The Federal Union—next to our liberty the most dear." [7]

The next year, 1831, Calhoun came out publicly as the leading nullificationist. And the year after that, Congress finally got around to revising the tariff, after repeated urging by the President. But the Tariff of 1832 did not lower the rates a great deal—certainly not enough to placate the South Carolina Radicals.

Now was the time, they thought, to put nullification to the test, and Calhoun agreed with them. In his Fort Hill Letter (August 28, 1832) he restated his argument that the state could, and he urged that the state at last should, "interpose" to protect its people. The people, he insisted, would have nothing to fear from the army or the navy, for nullification, he repeated, was by nature "peaceable, consistent with the federal relations of the State, and perfectly efficient, whether contested before the Courts, or attempted to be resisted by force." [8]

With Calhoun as their strategist and tactician, the Nullifiers, having got control of the legislature and the governorship, called a convention of delegates to represent the sovereign people of South Carolina. When it met, in November, the convention declared that all tariff acts, and particularly those of 1828 and 1832, were null and void within the state, from and after February 1, 1833. The anti-Nullifiers, who made up a large and respectable minority of the state's people, were powerless to stop the enthusiastic and almost hysterical onrush of the nullification majority.

To enable their top man to present their case in Washington, the Nullifiers elected Calhoun to the Senate seat that Hayne left in order to become governor. Now (December, 1832) Calhoun did something that nobody before or since has done: he resigned from the vice-presidency of the United States. He returned to Washington and took his new place (January 4, 1833) while the rumor ran that Jackson had sworn to hang him as a traitor. Jackson thought nullification was treason and, in a proclamation to the people of South Carolina, had told them so. He asked Congress for authority to use the army and the navy to enforce the laws, and Congress began to debate a Force Bill.

Calhoun found himself in a worrisome predicament. He and his South Carolina followers faced the threat of the nation's armed might, and they faced it by themselves. Though they had sympathizers in other states, no one of these states officially endorsed the South Carolina position. Not even Georgia stood by her sister state, though Georgia in a dispute with her Indian tribes had asserted her own version of state rights and was disregarding if not actually nullifying a decision of the United States Supreme Court. After getting rid of the Creeks, the state had undertaken also to remove the Cherokees and open their lands to white settlement. Chief Justice John Marshall, in two decisions (1831, 1832), held that the Indians were "domestic dependent nations" and exempt from Georgia laws. (Georgia, unlike South Carolina, had the President on her side; Jackson was quoted as saying with regard to the Georgia case: "John Marshall has made his decision; now let him enforce it.") The South Carolina Nullifiers gasconaded and called out troops, but they did not really dare to stand, alone, against the forces that Jackson could command.

Nevertheless, on the Senate floor, Calhoun bravely defended his state's action and denounced the Force Bill as unconstitutional. He also undertook to justify secession on constitutional grounds. He said a state could "*se*cede" from the Union as well as "*ac*cede" to it, as the states had done in 1787–88 and after. Webster rose to traverse Calhoun's arguments. There followed a Webster-Calhoun debate which, though less colorful and less celebrated than the Webster-Hayne debate three years earlier, exposed the issues far more thoroughly. Against Calhoun's subtle and intricate logic, Webster spoke as one dealing in plain matters of fact and common sense. "The truth is," he declared, "and no ingenuity of argument, no subtlety of distinction, can evade it, that, as to certain purposes, the people of the United States are one people." According to Webster, a state might secede from the Union, but it could do so only on the basis of the right of revolution, not on the basis of any constitutional right. While remaining within the Union, however, a state could not nullify congressional acts, for nullification was no right at all.[9]

From his plight Calhoun was to be saved not by his logic or eloquence but by the ingenuity of his old associate and rival, the Great Compromiser, Henry Clay. Already Congress was considering the Verplanck Bill, an Administration measure for immediately cutting the tariff and thus pacifying the country. Neither Calhoun nor Clay wished to see that bill pass, for its passage would redound to the credit of their mutual enemies the Jacksonians, especially Van Buren. So Clay introduced and Calhoun supported a different bill, a compromise tariff that would lower rates but would do so only gradually, over a ten-year period. This bill finally passed.

Jackson signed the Compromise Tariff and the Force Bill on the same day. Calhoun was satisfied, but would all his followers be? To justify his work he had hurried back to South Carolina and to the state convention, already reassembled. Most of its members were persuaded, now that Congress was repealing its obnoxious tariffs, to repeal their own ordinance nullifying those laws. But, as if to have the last word, the convention passed a new ordinance nullifying the Force Act!

This second ordinance—whatever might be said of the first—was merely a gesture. By now the Force Act was inoperative. It had been designed to take effect only if South Carolina resisted the collection of customs duties or otherwise violated federal law. Actually, the Nullifiers at no time attempted to interfere with the customs at Charleston or elsewhere, and after repealing their first ordinance they did not even threaten to interfere. In their second ordinance they nullified a law already null.

Calhoun claimed success for both of the nullification ordinances. "I have no doubt," he confided to a Northern friend, "the system has got its death wound," and he meant the protective system, the tariff. "Nullification has dealt the fatal blow. We have applied the same remedy to the bloody act," that is, the Force Act.[10] True, the tariff had been wounded, though not fatally by any means. And yet nullification had not really worked the way Calhoun had intended and had promised it would work. It had not been generally accepted as a legitimate and constitutional procedure —far from it. In practice the Calhoun principle had proved essentially a failure.

Though he never admitted this failure, Calhoun learned a lesson from it. He came to realize, only too well, that a single state, unaided, was powerless to interpose against federal authority. So, while retaining and even elaborating upon the nullification theory, he began to cultivate the condition he now knew was indispensable for the theory to operate. He began to cultivate, at every chance, a spirit of unity among all the Southern states. While not forgetting state rights, he gave more and more attention to fostering a sense of common sectional interests.

THE SECTIONALIST AND SLAVERY ADVOCATE

Slavery was—or could be made to be—the basis for unifying the South. Until the 1830's slavery often divided the South, which indeed had contained more antislavery societies than had the North. With the spread of cotton cultivation, however, the employment of slaves had become increasingly profitable. No more than one-fourth of the Southern whites ever owned slaves or belonged to slaveowning families, but most of the others aspired to become slaveowners, and the rest (who owned and desired no slaves) eventually came to believe that they too had a vital stake in the preservation of slavery. They were convinced by the "proslavery argument."

The year 1831 marked a turning point in the development of proslavery feeling in the South. On January 1, in Boston, appeared the first number of William Lloyd Garrison's *Liberator,* demanding immediate and uncompensated emancipation and striking a new note of urgency and extremism in the antislavery movement. That summer, in Southampton County, Virginia, occurred the Nat Turner insurrection, an uprising of slaves who slaughtered dozens of the masters and their wives and children before being bloodily put down. And that fall, at the meeting of the legislature in Richmond, the representatives of slaveless farmers from western Virginia demanded statewide emancipation; before the session was over they came remarkably close to achieving just that.

As these events of 1831 showed, slavery was being threatened not only by slaves themselves but also by abolitionists in the North and nonslaveholders in the South. In response to the signs of the times, the Southern states drastically tightened their slave codes, and the planters and their spokesmen undertook an elaborate and systematic justification of slavery.[11]

No one contributed more to the growing proslavery argument than did Calhoun. Himself a slaveowner, he took pride in his reputation for justice and kindliness to his slaves, though these attributes did not prevent him from ordering "30 lashes well laid on" in punishment of a recaptured runaway.[12] From the time he first put forth his nullification theory, in 1828, he was concerned with the defense of slavery. As he said in "The South Carolina Exposition," the tariff was merely the occasion for his state to assert its rights; the real cause was the potential danger to the "peculiar domestic institution of the Southern States." After 1833 he brought the slavery issue boldly to the front. By 1837 he could boast of slavery as "a good—a positive good," and could rejoice: "Many in the South once believed that it was a moral and political evil. That folly and delusion are gone." [13]

Not yet, however, did the slavery question divide the major parties along sectional lines. So long as Jackson remained in the White House, he and his policies provided the main partisan issues. Besides threatening actual war against South Carolina, Jackson made political war against the Bank of the United States, vetoing a bill to recharter the bank and then withdrawing the government's deposits from it. To Jacksonians the bank was a dangerous monopoly, a source of political corruption, a Whore of Babylon.

The things that Jackson did, or failed to do, brought

about a realignment of voters and politicians. His opponents banded together, though many of them had little in common except their opposition to him. They said he was highhanded, autocratic, a would-be monarch, King Andrew I, and so they called themselves Whigs after the party which, in England, historically had stood for limiting the powers of the king.

Throughout Jackson's second term (1833–37) Calhoun cooperated with the two foremost Whigs, Clay and Webster, in resisting what all three viewed as usurpations on the part of the President. But Calhoun never joined the Whig party; he led a proslavery, state-rights faction that retained its independence. His followers, fanatically loyal, included at least a few in every state, North as well as South, and the great majority in South Carolina. From 1833 on, his home state was his pocket borough. To emphasize their detachment from both parties, the Calhounites in the South Carolina legislature (which chose presidential electors without a popular ballot) gave the state's electoral vote, in 1836 as in 1832, to neither the Democratic nor the Whig candidate.

Calhoun began to have doubts about his alliance with the Whigs as the antislavery movement grew in numbers, noise, and influence throughout the North. At most, as he realized, the abolitionists (he made no distinction between them and other, less militant antislavery groups) never amounted to more than a small minority of the Northern people. They were inspired, he thought, by sheer fanaticism and nothing else. This, he came to believe, would soon have died out if the Whigs had not encouraged it, inadvertently, by teaching that the federal government possessed wide and expandable powers—thus suggesting to the fanatics that federal powers might be further expanded to make possible emancipation, at least by indirect means. And though relatively few, the fanatics were becoming po-

litically important, for both the Whigs and the Democrats of the North, almost evenly divided as the two
parties were, had a temptation to cater to the antislavery vote. The Whigs, it seemed to Calhoun, were
somewhat more inclined than the Democrats to yield
to this temptation.

If the abolitionists held the balance of power in the
North, the Calhounites could do the same thing in
the South and thus offset the antislavery influence in
national politics. This was part of the role that Calhoun
conceived for his followers. Another thing they could
do was, eventually, to help elect him President. To get
an electoral majority he would need the support of a
fairly solid South plus the backing of a part of the
divided North.

In the hope of uniting Southerners behind him and
his principles, Calhoun chose to make an issue of
antislavery activities, and he chose to do it boldly and
dramatically. The antislavery societies were filling the
mail with their propaganda and plying Congress with
memorials for the abolition of the interstate slave trade
and of slavery itself in the territories, the District of
Columbia, and other places under federal jurisdiction
(though not inside the slave states themselves; even
the abolitionists agreed that Congress had no constitutional power to touch a state's strictly "domestic" institutions). In 1836 Calhoun reported a bill—which
failed to pass—forbidding postmasters to receive or
deliver antislavery literature in those states with laws
prohibiting its circulation. He wanted the state and
not the federal officials to decide what mail the United
States postal system could lawfully handle. He also
urged, in vain, that the Senate reject all antislavery
petitions outright. Instead, the Senate adopted a procedure, essentially like the "gag rule" of the House,
for receiving such petitions but automatically tabling
them.

In taking such an extreme stand, Calhoun could hardly hope to win the Senate over, but he could and did hope to win the Southern people to his cause. He appealed to them to close ranks. "If we do not defend ourselves none will defend; if we yield we will be more and more pressed as we recede; and if we submit we will be trampled under foot," he said. "All we want is concert, to lay aside all party differences and unite with zeal and energy in repelling approaching dangers. Let there be concert of action, and we shall find ample means of security without resorting to secession or disunion." [14]

In thus choosing to meet the antislavery attack "at the frontier," Calhoun went against the advice of some of the Southern leaders, who preferred to play down the issue so long as the danger was neither imminent nor absolutely clear. These hesitant Southerners feared that a premature counteroffensive would antagonize and unite the North, to the disadvantage of the South. By his tactics Calhoun doubtless did do himself and the slavery cause as much harm as good.

Finally, in 1837, Calhoun abandoned his Whig allies, with whom he had defended the Bank of the United States against Jackson's assaults. He now began to support the Van Buren Administration in its plan to set up an Independent Treasury and thus "divorce" the government from the banking business. Two years later he rejoined the Democratic party.

There was much that he disliked about the party, including its name. He was himself no democrat, and he had little in common with the city workingmen to whom, among others, the party catered. That is, he had little in common with them except for the votes which they could cast and which he, in some future presidential election, might receive. In practice he was fond of "the people," including the workers. In principle he feared the "needy and corrupt" many, whom he expected to rise sooner or later in revolt against their betters, the rich and wellborn few. At heart he preferred the Whigs to the Democrats, the party of the rich to the party of the poor. The Whig party was, in one of its aspects, a coalition of Northern businessmen and Southern planters. Calhoun always desired an even closer and more inclusive alliance of planters and businessmen for protection against what he conceived to be their mutual foe—the rising class of factory laborers. But he wanted the alliance to be made *on his own terms,* on the principles of state sovereignty and nullification.[15] The Northern Whig leaders rejected his overtures, and the Whig party became increasingly "consolidationist" as well as abolitionist. So Calhoun turned back to the Democratic party as the lesser of the two evils.

The Democrats proved the more amenable to Calhoun's teachings with regard to slavery and state rights. In 1837, to test the opinion of the Northern people and politicians, he introduced a set of resolutions upholding state sovereignty, denouncing the abolitionists, and denying the right of citizens of any state to "intermeddle" with slavery *anywhere* or to prevent the acquisition of slave territory or the admission of slave states. Five of his seven resolutions were adopted, and all of them drew more Democratic than Whig support.

Again, by this test case Calhoun was trying to arouse and unify the South. As always he made it appear that he stood on the defensive as against the aggressions of the abolitionists. "They are more intent on our destruction than we for our own safety," he averred. "They mark and punish, by withholding their votes, and throwing them in the opposite scale, all who dare oppose them; while a feeling of indifference and inattention prevails on the part of the people of the slaveholding States." [16]

As he looked ahead to the election of 1840 Calhoun expected another victory for the Democrats. He predicted that the Whig party would not last long, for it was "too heterogeneous to hold together under the shock of defeat." [17] As things turned out, the Whigs, with "Tippecanoe and Tyler too," won the log-cabin-and-hard-cider campaign of 1840, but the party proved too heterogeneous to hold together in victory. Old Tippecanoe, the war hero William Henry Harrison, died a month after his inauguration, and the Virginia state-rights man John Tyler took Harrison's place. Clay and the Whigs read Tyler out of their party. Tyler depended on Calhoun, as Senate leader of the Democrats, to frustrate Clay's Whig program in the Senate.

The discomfiture and disorganization of the Whigs, Calhoun thought, heightened his own chances for election to the presidency on the Democratic ticket in 1844. Now, if ever, he began to think, was the time for him to run. "Apart from a sense of duty, and a desire to do all I can to carry the country and especially the South through their present difficulties," he wrote in September, 1841, well ahead of time, "I have no desire for the office." [18] Before the end of 1842 the South Carolina legislature accepted his resignation from the Senate and formally nominated him for the presidency. In 1843 Harper and Brothers published a sketch of his life, together with a collection of his speeches (but none of the earlier ones in which he had demanded a strong and active federal government). The sketch, a most flattering one, presented Calhoun as a statesman of the purest motives and rarest genius. He himself had written most of it and had endorsed the rest, though his name did not appear on the title page.[19] All his efforts, political and literary, proved unavailing; he was out of the running before convention time in 1844.

The preconvention favorite of the Democrats was

Van Buren, whom Calhoun now accused of "political treachery" to him. Van Buren, too, soon lost out. He tried to hedge himself with regard to Texas annexation, which had become the all-consuming issue. Jackson's old lieutenant, James K. Polk, spoke out frankly and strongly for annexation, was made the Democratic candidate, and carried the election over his Whig opponent, Clay.

President Tyler and the Democrats, including Calhoun, took the election returns as a mandate from the people for the immediate acquisition of Texas. And the task of annexation diplomacy fell to Calhoun when, early in 1844, Tyler appointed him Secretary of State.

Upon assuming his new office Calhoun found an unanswered letter from the British minister in Washington, who explained that his government, having abolished slavery in its own empire (1833), was ready to assist in abolishing it throughout the world. Calhoun wrote and sent a remarkable reply. The United States, he said, must frustrate the insidious aim of the British and, to do so, must get possession of Texas. Otherwise, Texas might be induced to emancipate its slaves and thus, by setting a bad example and by extending the free-soil border, might increase the difficulties of preserving slavery in the United States. But slavery must be preserved. It was the ideal institution, for slaves no less than masters. To clinch his point, Calhoun cited statistics from the latest federal census to show that feeblemindedness and insanity were more common among the free Negroes of the North than the slaves of the South.[20]

He did not intend this letter for publication. What he had said in it, of course, was no more extreme than other things he had been saying on the same subject in speeches to the Senate. His letter was in line with his policy of meeting all attacks at the frontier or even beyond the frontier. But, in this particular case, that policy might embarrass him in his efforts to get Texas. And so it did. Somehow a copy of the letter was obtained and published by the New York *Evening Post,* a newspaper favorable to Van Buren. Understandably, the letter convinced many Northerners that the annexation movement was a proslavery plot. They protested, and the Senate voted down the annexation treaty that Calhoun had negotiated with a Texan diplomat.

Before the end of Tyler's term as President and Calhoun's as Secretary of State, the annexationists achieved their object by means of a joint resolution instead of a treaty. Constitutionally, the joint resolution was a rather dubious device for such a purpose. It was certainly dubious from the point of view of a strict constructionist like Calhoun, yet he ignored his scruples and approved it. And in the circumstances, the annexation of Texas stirred up antislavery and free-soil sentiment in the North as nothing had done before.

Calhoun hoped to stay in the cabinet after the inauguration of Polk in March, 1845, but Polk preferred not to keep him. That fall, the South Carolina legislature returned him to the Senate, where he was to remain for the rest of his life. Physically, he was no longer his old self. For the next five years he wasted away with pulmonary tuberculosis. His rapid-fire manner of speech lost some of its staccato effect, but his spirit—and his eyes—burned as brightly as ever. Gradually he assumed that unearthly appearance to be seen in his most familiar portrait.

In 1845 he startled his state-rights followers when, in Memphis, he told a convention of Southern railroad enthusiasts that the federal government ought, in some instances at least, to encourage internal improvements. For a decade he had been interested in the construction of a railroad from Charleston to the Ohio Valley so as to cement the commercial as well as the political relations between the South and the West. Always before he had suggested only indirect aid from the federal government. The government, he had said, should cede the public lands to the states, and they in turn could make land grants in aid of canal, highway, and railroad construction and river and harbor improvements. Now he maintained that, by virtue of its power to regulate interstate commerce, Congress could provide directly for the development of interstate trade routes. In the Senate he proposed only that the government grant lands to encourage the building of railroads and canals. Even this much was not approved by Congress, and if it had been, no doubt President Polk would have vetoed it, just as he vetoed the general rivers and harbors improvement bill of 1846.

Calhoun differed with Polk also on other matters, and if he had continued as Secretary of State, he could not have cooperated with the President in all the latter's diplomatic undertakings. He considered Polk too bellicose regarding the Oregon dispute with Great Britain, though he approved the final settlement dividing the Oregon country along the forty-ninth parallel. He desired no war with Great Britain and none with Mexico either; he believed that Polk needlessly provoked hostilities with Mexico. Once the war was under way, Calhun favored a strictly defensive strategy. He criticized the war even at the risk of losing some of his popularity in the South. The basis for his opposition was this: he feared that victory would bring additional territories to the United States and thus intensify sectional and class conflict. "Mexico is to us the forbidden fruit," he cautioned; "the penalty of eating it would be to subject our institutions to political death." [21] Surely the South had little to gain, he thought, for most of the land to be taken from Mexico was ill suited to plantation slavery.

The sectional crisis he predicted was not long in

coming. Only a few months after the beginning of the war, a Pennsylvania Democrat, David Wilmot, introduced in Congress a resolution to exclude slavery from all the new territories to be acquired. Calhoun hoped that Southerners would rally to defeat the Wilmot Proviso. "If they regard their safety they must defeat it even if the union should be rent asunder," he wrote to his daughter. "I desire above all things to save the whole; but if that cannot be, to save the portion where Providence has cast my lot, at all events." [22] The Wilmot Proviso was to pass the House several times, but the Senate never.

The Senate, with the existing balance of free and slave states, constituted a refuge and a bastion for slaveholders. It would cease to do so, however, if slavery should be excluded from all the new territories, if only free states should be created from them. So Calhoun insisted upon equality for the South in both the Senate and the territories. He declared: "I am a Southern man and a slaveholder—a kind and merciful one, I trust—and none the worse for being a slaveholder. I say, for one, I would rather meet any extremity upon earth than give up one inch of our equality—one inch of what belongs to us as members of this great republic!" [23]

In the Treaty of Guadalupe Hidalgo, ending the Mexican War (February, 1848), the United States obtained California and all the territory that lay between California and Texas. Not this Mexican cession, however, but the Oregon country occasioned the first congressional struggle, in the summer of 1848, when a bill for organizing Oregon as a territory came up. No one expected slavery ever to take root in that latitude, but Oregon might set a precedent for other territories, and so the slave issue was as hotly argued as if free soil in Oregon were actually at stake.

During the Oregon debate four proposals were made

for dealing with slavery in the territories. One was the extreme Northern, free-soil view; namely, that Congress ought to prohibit slavery in all of them. Two were moderate, compromise proposals: either that the territories be divided between free and slave soil by an east-west line, or that the territorial legislatures or courts, once these were organized, be left to decide the question. The other was the extreme Southern, pro-slavery demand, that Congress permit and protect slavery in all the territories.

For this Southern view, Calhoun was the foremost spokesman. He reasoned that Congress had no discretionary power regarding the territories but only held them in trust for the states. As trustee, Congress must respect the property rights of the people of all the states—and above all the property right in slaves. Thus the South must be guaranteed equality, but even that was no longer enough, according to Calhoun. The "aggressions" of the North, by now, had gone too far. The Northern states must also silence their abolitionists. Calhoun was infuriated when, in reply to him, the new Senator from Illinois, Stephen A. Douglas, said it was "the speeches of Southern men, representing Slave States, going to an extreme, breathing a fanaticism as wild" as that of any antislavery leader, which stimulated abolitionism in the North.[24]

When Congress finally set up a territorial government for Oregon, with slavery prohibited there, Calhoun thought of calling a Southern convention to plan joint measures of self-defense for the slave states. He decided to wait until after the presidential election of 1848. Privately he preferred *"any respectable southern planter whatever to any man of northern birth and residence"* as the next President.[25] The Democratic candidate, Lewis Cass of Michigan, was a man of Northern birth and residence, and the Whig candidate, Zachary Taylor of Louisiana, was a respectable planter and slaveowner, though as a professional army man he had spent most of his life in the West. Calhoun considered campaigning openly for Taylor but concluded it would be unwise for him to shift back to cooperation with the Whigs.

In this election there was a third party of Free-Soil Democrats, successors of the Liberty party men and forerunners of the modern Republicans. The Free-Soil Democratic candidate was Van Buren, and he drew away from Cass enough votes to help give the victory to Taylor.

Once in office, Taylor disappointed and shocked his fellow slaveowners. The new President leaned for advice upon Senator William H. Seward, a leader of the antislavery Whigs in New York State. The gold rush had brought to California sufficient population for statehood, and Taylor proposed to Congress that California be admitted as a state without going through the usual territorial stages. He did not care whether the state was free or slave; as it happened, the Californians adopted a constitution prohibiting slavery. To accept California as a free state would be to upset the Senate balance. Incensed, Calhoun and other Southerners threatened to take their own states out of the Union if California were allowed to come in. So began the sectional crisis of 1849–50, the most serious such crisis up to that time.

Now came the final dramatic appearance of the "great triumvirate"—Clay, Webster, and Calhoun—in senatorial debate. Clay proposed his last compromise. Admit California as a free state, he said, but do so only in a general settlement of Northern and Southern grievances. Also organize Arizona and New Mexico as territories without any prohibition of slavery. Settle in favor of New Mexico her boundary dispute with Texas, but in return let the federal government take over the Texan public debt. Abolish the slave trade but guarantee slavery within the District of Columbia. And pass a new, drastic, effective federal fugitive-slave law, so as to ensure the return of runaways, who were being encouraged by the Underground Railway and by the "personal-liberty" laws (prohibiting state officials from aiding in the capture of fugitives) of several Northern states. Here, in Clay's proposed general settlement, were concessions to both North and South.

The concessions to the South were by no means enough to satisfy Calhoun. By March 4, 1850, he was ready with a speech, but when the day came he was too weak and feverish to deliver it, and sat wrapped up in flannels, gesticulating from time to time, while a colleague read it for him. The Union was endangered, Calhoun had written, by the antislavery agitation and the numerical preponderance of the North. This preponderance, he contended, had resulted from federal policies that discriminated in the North's favor. The only way to preserve the Union was to guarantee the security of the South within it. Runaway slaves must be returned, but more than that: the antislavery agitation must be stopped, and the South must be given complete equality in the territories. All this was familiar, for Calhoun had said it often enough before, but now he added something new: the Constitution must be amended so as to provide absolute protection for the South. In his address Calhoun did not describe the constitutional change he had in mind. It was the establishment of a dual presidency, with one President to be elected by the North and the other by the South, each President to have a veto on all federal legislation.

To the end Calhoun insisted that he favored union, not disunion. True enough, he favored union—at a price. And to Northerners it seemed the price had risen rather high. He did not think so, of course. He thought he was asking for no more than simple justice. "If you, who represent the stronger position," he told the Northerners, "cannot agree to settle . . . on the broad principle of justice and duty, say so; and let the States we both represent agree to separate and depart in peace. If you are unwilling we should depart in peace, tell us so, and we shall know what to do, when you reduce the question to submission or resistance." [26] In other words, the alternative to continued union on his terms was secession, and if that should be resisted, civil war.

Three days after the presentation of Calhoun's final terms, Webster rose to give his Seventh of March address. He tried to soothe feelings by saying the territorial issue was unreal, for geographical conditions in most of the territories were unsuited to slavery; it was already prohibited there by an ordinance of God, and so an act of Congress was unnecessary. He pled for toleration on both sides. He denied again that the Union could, constitutionally, be dissolved.

When Webster had finished, the ghostlike Calhoun managed to make himself heard with a few words of dissent: "No, Sir, the Union *can* be broken." Yes, said Webster, but only by *revolution*, not by any constitutional procedure. In a few minutes the two old antagonists, still respectful of one another, weary after a whole generation of debate, ceased their colloquy.[27]

Three weeks later, March 31, 1850, Calhoun lay dead. He did not live to see the passage of the Compromise of 1850 nor the events that followed during the next fifteen years: the rescues of fugitive slaves, the disruption of the Whig party, the adoption of the Kansas-Nebraska Act, the rise of the new Republican party, the Dred Scott decision, Bleeding Kansas, John Brown's raid, the split in the Democratic party, the election of Abraham Lincoln, the establishment of the

Confederacy, the firing on Fort Sumter, the defeat and ruin of the South.

"The South! The poor South!" Calhoun had exclaimed upon his deathbed.[28] Certainly he had meant well for his section, his homeland. Yet by his very efforts to preserve the way of life he loved, he had helped to prepare the way for its ultimate destruction. No man had done more than he to arouse the North, divide the national political parties (the best bonds of union and also the best means of defense for Southern interests), justify state sovereignty (on which secession and the Confederacy were to be based), and persuade Southerners that extreme measures were peaceful and constitutional when, as events were to demonstrate, such measures could lead only to war. In the desolated South of 1865 it could aptly have been said of Calhoun: if you seek his monument, look about you.

Calhoun also left another and more lasting monument: his theory of government and politics. An examination of this may show whether, as some of his latter-day admirers say, his theorizing makes him more important to our generation than to his own.

Part 2

THE THEORY OF GOVERNMENT

Calhoun's thoughts about government arose as by-products of his activities in politics. From 1828 to 1850 he expressed these thoughts or fragments of them in various reports, speeches, letters, and conversations. Finally he gave systematic expression to his thinking in two treatises, *A Disquisition on Government* and *A Discourse on the Constitution and Government of the United States*, which he began to write in 1843 but did not complete until shortly before his death; both were published posthumously. Though these two works summarize his theory, they must be supplemented by his other statements if it is to be fully and correctly understood. Moreover, all his writings must be viewed in the light of their historical backgrounds and their logical assumptions.

STATE-RIGHTS PRECEDENTS

State loyalty had roots trailing back to colonial times. The attachment of people to one colony and their antagonism toward other colonies prevented union when, in the face of common danger, Benjamin Franklin proposed his Albany Plan in 1754. The same sentiments hampered intercolonial cooperation during the French and Indian War which ensued. "Fire and water are not more heterogeneous than the different colonies in North America. Nothing can exceed the jealousy and emulation which they possess in regard to each other."

So wrote, with some exaggeration, the Englishman Andrew Burnaby, who traveled through the middle settlements in 1759 and 1760. He thought the colonies differed so much in character, manners, religion, and material interest that "were they left to themselves, there would even be a civil war." [1]

Hostility to the imperial government brought the colonies together in 1774 and held them together, as independent states, during the Revolutionary War. Their rivalries, however, delayed the adoption of the Articles of Confederation until 1781, and the second of these Articles affirmed: "Each state retains its sovereignty, freedom and independence, and every Power, Jurisdiction and right, which is not by this confederation expressly delegated to the United States, in Congress assembled." The states retained, among other things, the power to tax. All had to approve before the Articles could be amended, and all but one did approve an amendment for a tariff, which therefore failed to be adopted.

Alexander Hamilton and other "nationalists" undertook to replace this form of government, so weak and so difficult to strengthen. They finally succeeded at the Philadelphia constitutional convention, 1787–88, which had been called to revise the Articles but which chose to discard them and start afresh. The resulting plan of government was, as its "father," James Madison, said, "in strictness, neither a national nor a federal Constitution, but a composition of both." [2] Certainly it embodied a number of compromises between nationalist and state-right views, and it evaded a number of issues that might have prevented any agreement. Still, the new Constitution as drawn up in Philadelphia was more nationalist than otherwise, and for that reason the Antifederalists (who were really antinationalists) opposed its ratification.

Drawn up by delegates from the various states, meeting in a single convention, the document was ratified by other delegates meeting in separate state conventions. It was to go into effect among the ratifying states when nine of them had acted, and before the end of 1788 eleven did so; the other two (North Carolina and Rhode Island) still held out. Some had ratified only after a close contest and only on the understanding that certain amendments soon would be added. The two holdouts waited to see what would happen. All were satisfied by the ten amendments proposed by the new Congress at its first session. These amendments further limited the powers of the government, and the tenth provided: "The powers not delegated to the United States by the Constitution, nor prohibited by it to the States, are reserved to the States respectively, or to the people." Thus amended, the Constitution was more nearly balanced as between national and federal tendencies—and more ambiguous.

It could be interpreted in opposite ways. In its clause giving Congress all powers "necessary and proper" for carrying the specified powers into effect, Alexander Hamilton as Secretary of the Treasury found ample authorization for his financial program, including a national bank. In the Tenth Amendment Thomas Jefferson as Secretary of State discovered a bar to congressional legislation of that kind; no power to establish a bank having been delegated to Congress, that power must have been reserved to the states. As President, George Washington sided with Hamilton and signed the bills that Congress passed to put Hamilton's recommendations into effect. Eventually Jefferson withdrew from the Administration and, with Madison, organized an opposition to it. Thus, in the 1790's, originated the two parties, Federalist and Republican, the one willing to exploit the "implied powers" of the Constitution, the other demanding a "strict construction" of the document.

The Republicans, already convinced that much of
the Federalist legislation was unconstitutional, were
further outraged when, in 1798, Congress passed the
Alien and Sedition Acts. The Sedition Act—for fining
and imprisoning those who uttered anything "false,
scandalous, and malicious" against the government, the
Congress, or the President—seemed flagrantly to violate
the First Amendment, which stated that Congress
should pass no law abridging freedom of speech or of
the press.

What agency should decide the question of constitutionality? The Constitution did not, in so many words,
give the Supreme Court power to decide, and the Republicans denied that the Court could rightfully assume the power. Their leaders, Jefferson and Madison,
concluded that the state legislatures should decide, and
they ably expressed their view in two sets of resolutions, one written (anonymously) by Jefferson and
adopted by the Kentucky legislature (1798–99), and
the other drafted by Madison and approved by the Virginia legislature (1798).

These Kentucky and Virginia resolutions asserted
the following doctrines: The federal government had
been formed by a "compact" or contract among the
states. It was a limited government, possessing only
certain delegated powers. Whenever it attempted to
exercise any additional and undelegated powers, its
acts were "unauthoritative, void, and of no force." The
parties to the contract, the states, must decide for
themselves when and whether the central government
exceeded its powers. The state legislatures must serve
as "sentinels" to watch out for unconstitutional acts.
And "nullification" by the states was the "rightful
remedy" whenever the general government went too
far. The resolutions urged all the states to join in declaring the Alien and Sedition Acts null and void and
in requesting their repeal at the next session of Con-

gress, but none of the others went along with Virginia and Kentucky.

State rights and strict construction were usually the arguments of the party out of power (and so they were to be throughout American history). So long as the Republicans were the *outs,* they remained strict constructionists, but once they had become the *ins,* with Jefferson as President, they used the full powers of the federal government to further the agrarian interest they represented. Indeed, they used much more than the rightful and constitutional powers, according to the Federalists. The Federalists now adopted the state-rights point of view.

The Republicans bought Louisiana from France (1803) even though the Constitution gave Congress no explicit power to acquire new territory. On the constitutionality of the purchase Jefferson himself had serious doubts but managed to overcome them. The Republicans also imposed an embargo (1808) forbidding American ships to leave American ports, though the Constitution had given Congress authority only to regulate interstate commerce, not to prohibit it. In anger against the Louisiana Purchase, a few extreme Federalists, the Essex Junto, conspired to bring about the secession of New England. In denouncing the embargo, a much larger number resorted to doctrines of state rights. The young New Hampshire Federalist Daniel Webster, for one, paraphrased the Virginia and Kentucky resolutions: "The Government of the United States is a delegated, *limited* Government." [3]

During the presidency of Jefferson's intimate friend and successor, James Madison, the New England state-rights men gained their largest following, in opposition to the War of 1812. In Congress, Webster attacked and helped to defeat a conscription bill. "The operation of measures thus unconstitutional and illegal ought to be prevented by a resort to other measures which are both constitutional and legal," he declared, hinting at nullification by New Hampshire. "It will be the solemn duty of the state governments to protect their own authority over their own militia and to interpose between their citizens and arbitrary power." [4] In fact, some of the New England states, by refusing to support the war, virtually nullified the war effort of the federal government. New England state-rightism and sectionalism reached a climax in the Hartford Convention (1814-15), which demanded changes in the Constitution and threatened secession in case the changes were not made.

Some of Jefferson's followers had turned against him on the ground that he departed from his own principles. His distant cousin and (before 1804) House leader, John Randolph of Roanoke, organized within the Republican party a state-rights faction known as the Quids. Randolph remained a fanatical defender of Virginia rights, and he criticized Calhoun among others for aggrandizing the government in Washington. John Taylor, of Caroline, an equally consistent but more original thinker than Randolph, led the "Virginia school" (including St. George Tucker and Spencer Roane) in rationalizing resistance to the centralizing trend, especially to the work of the Supreme Court under that other Virginian, John Marshall. After his retirement from the presidency, Jefferson joined in opposing the Federalist-minded judges as "sappers and miners" who were undermining the Constitution. The Georgia state-rights men, whose national leader was William H. Crawford, Calhoun's onetime rival for the presidency, had their own quarrel with Marshall and the Court over the question of the Georgia Indians. [5]

Thus, by the time Calhoun took up the state-rights doctrine, in 1828, he was a late-comer to the cause. Already it had many precedents. With the more important of these he could not help being familiar. He was the son of an Antifederalist and Republican of the early strict-constructionist kind. He attended Yale College and the Litchfield law school at a time when these were centers of the Federalist phase of state-rights thinking. In Congress he heard the arguments of Webster and others who decried the nationalistic measures, which he himself so stoutly championed, for winning the War of 1812. Afterward he was often enough reminded of the state-rights position by his critics, such men as John Randolph. He was schooled by current events.

ASSUMPTIONS: GOVERNMENT AND MAN

Calhoun read deeply and, within the limits of his taste, widely. For fiction, poetry, or other forms of belles-lettres he cared little; he preferred the more solid studies of history and politics, ancient and modern. At one time or another he looked into the writings of his state-rights predecessors like Jefferson, Madison, Taylor, Tucker, and Thomas Cooper, an antitariff economist and president of the College of South Carolina. He studied the English theorist who, more than any other author, influenced the Jeffersonians—John Locke. He also made himself acquainted with the oratory of Demosthenes and Cicero, the history of Polybius, the politics of Machiavelli and Algernon Sidney, the philosophy of Thomas Hobbes, and the economics of Adam Smith. Most of all he perused and reperused the works of Aristotle and Edmund Burke, his favorites.[6]

Though he learned from many men, Calhoun remained the disciple of none. An eclectic, he culled the thoughts of each, picking out those he could use in constructing his own system of ideas. From Jefferson and Madison, for example, he took clues to nullification but no commitment to human equality and natural rights. From Locke he accepted the labor theory of value (the theory that property acquired its worth and men their title to it from the labor they put into it) and from Hobbes the notion of self-interest as the main motive of political man. He rejected the belief, which Locke and Hobbes shared, that government had originated in a contract among men who previously lived in an anarchic "state of nature." He possessed too strong a sense of historical continuity and societal hierarchy—a sense for which he got confirmation from Aristotle and Burke—to believe that people ever had existed or could exist without society and government to keep them in order.

The reason for the existence of government he found in human nature. "I assume," he wrote, in his *Disquisition on Government*, "that man is so constituted as to be a social being. His inclinations and wants, physical and moral, irresistibly impel him to associate with his kind; and he has, accordingly, never been found, in any age or country, in any state other than the social." Man, by his nature, always has lived in society and, by his nature, always has required government, for while interested in others he is even more interested in himself. He is "so constituted as to feel more intensely what affects him directly than what affects him indirectly through others; or, to express it differently, he is so constituted that his direct or individual affections are stronger than his sympathetic or social feelings. I intentionally avoid the expression *selfish* feelings . . . because . . . it implies an unusual excess of the individual over the social feelings . . . and, consequently, something depraved and vicious." Even the usual excess of self-interested over social feelings "necessarily leads to conflict between individuals."

Each, in consequence, has a greater regard for his

own safety or happiness than for the safety or happiness of others and, where these come in opposition, is ready to sacrifice the interests of others to his own. And hence the tendency to a universal state of conflict between individual and individual, accompanied by the connected passions of suspicion, jealousy, anger, and revenge—followed by insolence, fraud, and cruelty—and, if not prevented by some controlling power, ending in a state of universal discord and confusion, destructive of the social state and the ends for which it is ordained. This controlling power, wherever vested or by whomsoever exercised, is GOVERNMENT.

If man is to develop his intellectual and moral faculties, and thus perfect society, he must, according to Calhoun, have both liberty and security, and he must have an appropriate balance between the two. Too much liberty would mean too little security. How much liberty may safely be allowed depends upon physical conditions, such as the defensibility of borders and the nearness of potential enemies, but even more upon moral considerations, such as the intelligence, virtue, and patriotism of the mass of the people, and their experience and proficiency in the art of self-government. "A community may possess all the necessary moral qualifications in so high a degree as to be capable of self-government under the most adverse circumstances; while, on the other hand, another may be so sunk in ignorance and vice as to be incapable of forming a conception of liberty or of living, even when most favored by circumstances, under any other than an absolute and despotic government." Liberty, in short, is not a natural right but a social reward, something to be earned and deserved. "It is a great and dangerous error to suppose that all people are equally entitled to liberty."

It is also a great and dangerous error, Calhoun averred, to assume that liberty and equality go together. The equality of citizens in the eyes of the law, yes, but not the equality of people in economic, social, or political condition. Liberty leads to inequality, and inequality is essential to progress.

In order to understand why this is so, it is necessary to bear in mind that the main spring to progress is the desire of individuals to better their condition; and that the strongest impulse which can be given to it is to leave individuals free to exert themselves in the manner they may deem best for that purpose, as far at least as it can be done consistently with the ends for which government is ordained, and to secure to all the fruits of their exertions. Now, as individuals differ greatly from each other, in intelligence, sagacity, energy, perseverance, skill, habits of industry and economy, physical power, position and opportunity, the necessary effect of leaving all free to exert themselves to better their condition must be a corresponding inequality between those who may possess these qualities and advantages in a high degree, and those who may be deficient in them. The only means by which this result can be prevented are either to impose such restrictions on the exertions of those who may possess them in a high degree, as will place them on a level with those who do not; or to deprive them of the fruits of their exertions. But to impose such restrictions on them would be destructive of liberty—while to deprive them of the fruits of their exertions would be to destroy the desire of bettering their condition. It is, indeed, this inequality of condition between the front and rear ranks, in the march of progress, which gives so strong an impulse to the former to maintain their position and to the latter to press forward into their files. This gives to progress its greatest impulse. To force the front rank back to the rear, or attempt to push forward the rear into line with the front, by the interposition of the government, would put an end to the impulse and effectually arrest the march of progress.[7]

Calhoun thought these ideas of natural liberty and equality were dangerous because they gave rise to revolutionary discontents, at home and abroad, and to abolitionism. If disunion and civil war should ever come to America, he believed, the origins could be traced to those ideas. And he insisted the ideas were false; they were merely reflections of the "hypothetical truism" that "all men are born free and equal." This proposition he attacked again and again, as in a Senate speech of 1848:

Taking the proposition literally (it is in that sense it is to be understood), there is not a word of truth in it. It begins with "all men are born," which is utterly untrue. Men are not born. Infants are born. They grow to be men. And concludes with asserting that they are born "free and equal," which is not less false. They are not born free. While infants they are incapable of freedom, being destitute alike of the capacity of thinking and acting, without which there can be no freedom.

Besides, they are necessarily born subject to their parents, and remain so among all people, savage and civilized, until the development of their intellect and physical capacity enables them to take care of themselves. They grow to all the freedom of which the condition in which they are born permits, by growing to be men. Nor is it less false that they are born "equal." They are not so in any sense in which it can be regarded; and thus, as I have asserted, there is not a word of truth in the whole proposition, as expressed and generally understood.

If we trace it back, we shall find the proposition differently expressed in the Declaration of Independence. That asserts that "all men are created equal." The form of expression, though less dangerous, is not less erroneous. All men are not created. According to the Bible, only two—a man and a woman—ever were, and of these one was pronounced subordinate to the other. All others have come into the world by being born, and in no sense, as I have shown, either free or equal. . . .

If the proposition be traced still further back, it will be found to have been adopted from certain writers on government who had attained much celebrity in the early settlement of these States, and with whose writings all the prominent actors in our revolution were familiar. Among these, Locke and Sydney were prominent. But they expressed it very differently. According to their expression, "all men in the state of nature were free and equal." From this the others were derived. . . .

Man, for the purpose of reasoning, may be regarded . . . in a state of individuality. . . . It is certain that . . . the very supposition that he lived apart and separated from all others would make him free and equal. No one in such a state could have the right to command or control another. Every man would be his own master and might do just as he pleased. But it is equally clear that man cannot exist in such a state; that he is by nature social, and that society is necessary not only to the proper development of all his faculties, moral and intellectual, but to the very existence of his race.[8]

These assumptions regarding man and his relation to society and government provided a foundation for the logical structure that Calhoun erected. Not that he began with the base and worked up. Not that he turned, in 1828, to constructing his theory because, at that time, he happened to receive an insight into human nature. Rather, he started with a practical problem—how to protect the interests of his state and section without losing his own opportunities in politics—and he proceeded over the years to develop political techniques and intellectual justifications for them. While doing so he undertook to give logical consistency to his thought as a whole. Eventually he discovered the human traits that seemed to make government necessary in the first place and furnished criteria for deciding whether, once established, a particular government was good or bad.

"It follows," he concluded, "that the more perfectly a government combines power and liberty—that is, the greater its power and the more enlarged and secure the liberty of individuals—the more perfectly it fulfills the ends for which government is ordained." [9] In the task of reconciling power and liberty he saw what is indeed the basic dilemma of any democratic or representative government. And to this task he directed himself in devising his own version of political science with its principle of the "concurrent majority," its procedure for nullification, and all the rest.

THE CONCURRENT MAJORITY

Though intended to protect and preserve society, government "has itself a strong tendency to disorder and abuse of its powers," Calhoun wrote, "as all experience and almost every page of history testify." The cause for this he found in the same elements of human nature that made government indispensable. Governments are run by men, and men are impelled by self-interest. Those in power naturally will oppress and exploit the rest of the community unless prevented. "That by which this is prevented, by whatever name called, is what is meant by CONSTITUTION, in its most comprehensive sense, when applied to GOVERNMENT." A constitution, any constitution, is in other words the means by which the powers of government are limited and controlled.

An adequate constitution must provide more than mere paper guarantees of the rights of the governed. "Power can only be resisted by power—and tendency by tendency. Those who exercise power and those subject to its exercise—the rulers and the ruled—stand in antagonistic relations to each other." The ruled can be expected to resist the rulers if there is a means of peaceable and effective resistance. "Such an organization, then, as will furnish the means by which resistance may be systematically and peaceably made on the part of the ruled, to oppression and abuse of power on the part of the rulers, is the first and indispensable step towards *forming* a constitutional government."

The primary principle of such an organization is the right of suffrage, the right of the ruled to choose their rulers from time to time. This right alone, however, is not enough. "The right of suffrage, of itself, can do no more than give complete control to those who elect, over the conduct of those they have elected." These become merely the agents of the group or groups that elected them. If all groups had the same interests, if all were affected exactly alike by governmental action, then the right to vote would sufficiently counteract the government's tendency to exceed its powers. But such is not the case. Any community, especially a far-flung, rich, and populous one, is divided into groups with differing and conflicting interests. Each group, or interest,

desires to get control of the government so as to protect and promote its ends. "If no one interest be strong
enough, of itself, to obtain it, a combination will be
formed between those whose interests are most alike—
each conceding something to the others until a sufficient number is obtained to make a majority." And "the
dominant majority, for the time, would have the same
tendency to oppression and abuse of power which,
without the right of suffrage, irresponsible rulers would
have." [10]

So, if there is to be a true constitution, it must contain another principle in combination with the right of
suffrage. This other provision "must be of a character
calculated to prevent any one interest or combination
of interests from using the powers of government to
aggrandize itself at the expense of the others."

There is but one certain mode in which this result
can be secured, and that is by the adoption of
some restriction or limitation which shall so effectively prevent any one interest or combination of
interests from obtaining the exclusive control of
the government as to render hopeless all attempts
directed to that end. There is, again, but one mode
in which this can be effected; and that is by taking
the sense of each interest or portion of the community, which may be unequally and injuriously
affected by the action of the government, separately, through its own majority, or in some other way
by which its voice may be fairly expressed; and to
require the consent of each interest either to put
or to keep the government in action. This, too, can
be accomplished only in one way, and that is by
such an organism of the government—and, if necessary for the purpose of the community also—as
will, by dividing and distributing the powers of
government, give to each division or interest,

through its appropriate organ, either a concurrent voice in making and executing the laws or a veto on their execution. It is only by such an organism that the assent of each can be made necessary to put the government in motion, or the power made effectual to arrest its action when put in motion, and it is only by one or the other that the different interests, orders, classes, or portions, into which the community may be divided, can be protected, and all conflict and struggle between them pre-vented—by rendering it impossible to put or keep it in action without the concurrent consent of all.

Thus there are two ways, both of them indispensa-ble for constitutional government, to take the "sense of the community," and each of them indicates the will of the majority. One of the two, however, "regards num-bers only and considers the whole community as a unit having but one common interest throughout." The other "regards interests as well as numbers," considers the community "as made up of different and conflict-ing interests," and "takes the sense of each" and "the united sense of all." The former, Calhoun called "the numerical or absolute majority" and the latter, "the concurrent or constitutional majority."

Government without the concurrent majority, he went on to say, is always absolute government. It makes no difference whether the government be demo-cratic, aristocratic, or monarchic, for the essential point is the existence of *"one power"* and not the *"number,"* few or many, in whom that power may be vested. The numerical majority may be just as tyrannical as any dictator, any king. Indeed, when the distinction be-tween the numerical and the concurrent majority is overlooked, as it commonly is, a democratic govern-ment tends readily to degenerate into out-and-out dic-tatorship.

Every constitutional government, Calhoun insisted, has some arrangement for a "mutual negative" among the various conflicting interests in the community. "It is this negative power, the power of preventing or arresting the action of the government—be it called by what term it may: veto, interposition, nullification, check, or balance of power—which, in fact, forms the constitution."

To the uninitiated, such a negative power might seem to weaken if not destroy the government, but not to Calhoun. He thought the "conservative principle" (or preservative principle) of government by concurrent majority was more efficient than that of government by numerical majority. "This principle in constitutional governments is *compromise*—and in absolute governments is *force*." All the interests could protect themselves by the device of the concurrent majority.

> Its effect, then, is to cause the different interests, portions, or orders, as the case may be, to desist from attempting to adopt any measure calculated to promote the prosperity of one or more by sacrificing that of others; and thus to force them to unite in such measures only as would promote the prosperity of all, as the only means to prevent the suspension of the action of the government and, thereby, to avoid anarchy, the greatest of all evils.[11]

That is to say, the very requirement of unanimity would make all groups more forbearing, more cooperative, and thus would strengthen and preserve the government without resort to force, which could only lead to the destruction of constitutional government. On the concurrent majority as the key to union, Calhoun waxed almost lyrical, outlining a sort of Utopia:

By giving to each interest or portion the power of self-protection, all strife and struggle between them for ascendency is prevented; and, thereby, not only every feeling calculated to weaken the attachment to the whole is suppressed, but the individual and the social feelings are made to unite in one common devotion to country. Each sees and feels that it can best promote its own prosperity by conciliating the goodwill and promoting the prosperity of the others. And hence there will be diffused throughout the whole community kind feelings between its different portions; and, instead of antipathy, a rivalry amongst them to promote the interests of each other, as far as this can be done consistently with the interest of all. Under the combined influence of these causes, the interests of each would be merged in the common interests of the whole; and thus the community would become a unit, by becoming the common centre of attachment of all its parts. And hence, instead of faction, strife, and struggle for party ascendency, there would be patriotism, nationality, harmony, and a struggle only for supremacy in promoting the common good of the whole.

"When something *must* be done, and when it can be done only by the united consent of all," Calhoun was confident, "the necessity of the case will force to a compromise, be the cause of that necessity what it may." By way of illustration he offered the familiar example of trial by jury. Here twelve men, chosen more or less at random, must concur unanimously in order to reach a verdict. To someone unacquainted with jury trials, the procedure would seem to be utterly impracticable. Yet it worked. The jurors, knowing they must all agree, listened to the arguments on both sides and consulted one another under the influence of a *"disposition to harmonize."*

Governing a country by concurrent majority, Calhoun believed, was equally feasible. He searched history for examples and thought he found an excellent one in the case of Poland, where the principle of the "negative power" was carried to extremes in the *liberum veto.* As he described the system, the election of the Polish kings required "the concurrence or acquiescence of every individual of the nobles and gentry present, in an assembly numbering usually from one hundred and fifty to two hundred thousand." So also the procedure of the Polish diet, or legislature, permitted a veto by any of its members, "thus making an unanimous vote necessary to enact a law or to adopt any measure whatever." If such a government had never existed, Calhoun said, it would have been thought too awkward to work and too feeble to last. "And yet this government lasted, in this form, more than two centuries, embracing the period of Poland's greatest power and renown." (Historians nowadays do not agree with Calhoun that the *liberum veto* actually worked as it was supposed to or that it was a source of strength to Poland.)

He discovered an example closer to home in the Confederacy of the Six Nations—the Iroquois—who once inhabited the western part of the state of New York. Each nation chose one delegate, who in turn picked six associates; these forty-two men, meeting in council, constituted the general or federal government of the tribes. Every one of the forty-two possessed a veto. "But this, instead of making the Confederacy weak or impracticable, had the opposite effect," Calhoun maintained. "It secured harmony in council and action, and with them a great increase of power." [12]

Still closer to home was the example of his own state, South Carolina, whose government embodied at least one feature of the concurrent majority. Originally the low-country planters had dominated both branches of the state legislature. The frontiersmen and farmers of the upcountry protested more and more as they increased in numbers. Finally, by a compromise in 1807, the system of apportionment was changed so that the low country controlled the Senate and the upcountry the House. Thereafter all legislation required the concurrence of both parts of the state. "The consequence was the almost instantaneous restoration of harmony and concord between the two sections." [13]

Calhoun believed, however, that his principle was best exemplified by the government of ancient Rome and by that of Great Britain—"the two most remarkable and perfect of their respective forms of constitutional governments." He gathered from his study of history that the Roman people had consisted of two distinct orders, or classes—the Patricians and the Plebeians. At one time the government was under the control of the Patricians alone. After an accumulation of grievances, the Plebeians threatened to revolt, with the army on their side. The Patricians sent commissioners to treat with the army. The upshot was a "formal compact" between the two orders giving the Plebeians the right to elect two tribunes as the protectors of their order. Later the number of tribunes was increased to ten, who were chosen by separate tribes. Thus, through the tribunes, the Plebeians gained a veto on the passage and the execution of all laws.

By this arrangement, the government was placed under the concurrent and joint voice of the two orders, expressed through separate and appropriate organs, the one possessing the positive and the other the negative powers of the government. This simple change converted it from an absolute into a constitutional government—from a government of the patricians only to that of the whole Roman people—and from an aristocracy into a republic. In doing this, it laid the solid foundation of Roman liberty and greatness.

Rome developed greater power than Great Britain or any other community ever did, according to Calhoun. "But the British government is far superior to that of Rome in its adaptation and capacity to embrace under its control extensive dominions without subverting its constitution." The British realm consisted of three estates: the king, the lords temporal and spiritual, and the commons. The king not only headed the realm but also represented *the tax-consuming interest* or, more broadly, the great interest which necessarily grows out of the action of the government, be its form what it may—the interest that *lives by the government.*" The House of Commons "is the head and representative of the opposite—the great tax-paying interest, by which the government is supported." Between king and commons there is necessarily a strong and constant tendency to conflict.

To prevent this, the House of Lords, as one of the estates of the realm, is interposed and constitutes the conservative power of the government. It consists, in fact, of that portion of the community who are the principal recipients of the honors, emoluments, and other advantages derived from the government, and whose condition cannot be improved but must be made worse by the triumph of either of the conflicting estates over the other; and hence it is opposed to the ascendency of either and in favor of preserving the equilibrium between them.

The three orders, king, lords, and commons, "are blended in the legislative department, so that the separate and concurring act of each is necessary to make laws." [14]

Unlike ancient Rome or modern Britain, France lacked a constitutional government and, in Calhoun's belief, lacked the conditions prerequisite to its formation. When he first received news of the French Revolution of 1848, he wrote: "France is not prepared to become a Republick." As the months passed he remained sure that the effort to set up a "free popular Government" there would fail. It was bound to fail because France had "no elements out of which such a government could be formed" and, even if she had them, "still she must fail from her total misconception of the principles on which such a government, to succeed, must be constructed." That is, France was not a confederation of separate states or estates, and she was infected with "this radical and most dangerous of all errors," that liberty is a natural right. Calhoun predicted, accurately enough, that the revolutionary movement in France would lead to "distraction, anarchy and finally absolute power, in the hand of one man."

He expected similar results in all but one of the revolution-torn countries on the continent of Europe. He had higher hopes for Germany. In Germany there existed the proper "materials" and possibly the correct spirit. "Nothing but woful experience can apply a remedy," he wrote, "except perhaps in Germany, where the advantage of an existing system of confederation of states, and the dread of France from the experience of the first revolution, may lead to establish a federal system somewhat like ours." [15]

Our federal system, he believed, was originally intended to operate on the right principle, with suitable arrangements for the negative power. There was, after all, the *division of powers* between the state governments and the federal government. Within the federal government there was the *separation of powers* as between the executive, legislative, and judiciary branches, and there was the further separation as between the two legislative bodies, the Senate and the House of Representatives. The members of the House were elected by popular constituencies in proportion to numbers, but the Senators were chosen by the state legislatures, two from each state, regardless of its population. The judges were appointed by the President with the consent of the Senate, and the President was supposed to be picked by a college of electors appointed or elected from the states. Terms of office varied from two years for congressmen to life for judges. Surely, with its complex system of officeholding, its numerous checks and balances, and its division of powers, the Constitution of the Americans, though unique, was designed as a true constitution comparable to that of the Poles, the Iroquois, the Romans, or the British. Calhoun thought so.

Yet, he believed, the government in actual practice did not work as it was intended and designed to. One reason was the failure of Americans to understand and appreciate the inwardness of their own Constitution. Another was the growth of political parties. The party of the numerical majority could get control of the presidency, the Supreme Court, both houses of Congress, and most of the state governments, all at the same time. Then the checks and balances could not avail to prevent the numerical majority from exploiting the rest of the community. The press and public opinion would not, as some Americans argued, provide a substitute check, for the newspapers only reflected the will of the numerical majority.[16]

Before the end of his life Calhoun concluded that the preponderance of the North (the numerical majority) had gone so far as to make necessary a change in the Constitution. He conceived his plan for an amendment setting up a dual presidency, one President to be elected from the free states, the other from the slave states. The two might divide the executive duties between them in various ways; for instance, one might take charge of domestic and the other of foreign affairs. That was unimportant. The important thing was that each of the two would have a veto on all legislation. Thus the second President would serve as the tribune of the South.[17]

Throughout most of his career as a state-rights logician, however, Calhoun remained satisfied that the principle of the concurrent majority was adequately embodied in the Constitution itself. All he had to do was to point out the principle and the procedure for putting it into action. That procedure was nullification.

NULLIFICATION

Calhoun based his idea of nullification upon a concept of "state sovereignty." The term "sovereignty" refers to the ultimate authority or source of power within a body politic, but the term has been defined and used in a variety of ways. It originated with the appearance of nation-states in the early modern period, and it was then intended to justify the power of the rising kings. In the sixteenth century the pioneer French political scientist Jean Bodin defined it as the "highest power over citizens and subjects, unrestrained by laws"; he considered it essentially indivisible as well as illimitable. In the seventeenth and eighteenth centuries the Englishmen Thomas Hobbes and William Blackstone elaborated upon the doctrine of sovereignty as something undivided and uncontrolled. The *Commentaries* of Blackstone became the leading textbook for American students of law.

In the eighteenth and early nineteenth centuries, however, few Americans adopted the Blackstone view of sovereignty. At first, indeed, few Americans used the term at all, and when they did use it, they thought of sovereignty as residing, if it resided anywhere, in the people and not in a ruler. Though the term appears in the Articles of Confederation, it is nowhere to be found in either the Declaration of Independence or the United States Constitution. Most of the Founding Fathers believed that government was limited by natural law and natural rights, and so these men could see no place for absolute and unrestricted authority. Furthermore, they faced the delicate task of planning a strong government yet obtaining approval for it from the jealous states, and so they preferred to evade the question of the location of sovereignty—the question whether ultimate power came from the peoples of the several states or from the people of the country as a whole.

James Madison did not evade the question. He explained that the Constitution provided for an unprecedented kind of government to which old concepts did not apply. He believed that sovereignty could be both divided and limited, for it meant nothing more than the power of government. This was not an absolute power: individuals retained natural rights that were "beyond the legitimate reach of sovereignty, wherever vested and however viewed." Nor was it an absolute unit: one of the American states could be divided, as Virginia was when Kentucky became a separate state, and two sovereignties thus could be created where there had been only one before. As for the Constitution, "in the sources from which the ordinary powers of government are drawn, it is partly federal and partly national." Through the adoption of the Constitution, as Madison saw the matter, the states had given up parts of their sovereignty and had kept other parts.

In the early nineteenth century both the state-rights men, such as St. George Tucker, and the nationalists, such as John Marshall and Daniel Webster, assumed that sovereignty was divisible and, in the United States, was divided. "In America," to quote Marshall, "the powers of sovereignty are divided between the government of the Union and those of the states. They are each sovereign, with respect to the objects committed to them." [18] Like most of his American contemporaries, Marshall did not distinguish clearly between *sovereignty* and *governmental powers*. But Calhoun did.

To Calhoun, the idea of divided sovereignty was absurd. He wrote:

> There is no difficulty in understanding how powers, appertaining to sovereignty, may be divided; and *the exercise* of one portion delegated to one set of agents, and another portion to another; or how sovereignty may be vested in one man, or in a few, or in many. But how sovereignty itself, the supreme power, can be divided—how the people of the several States can be partly sovereign and partly *not* sovereign, partly supreme and partly *not* supreme—it is impossible to conceive. Sovereignty is an entire thing; to divide is to destroy it.

To Calhoun, it seemed equally ridiculous to suppose that sovereignty ever had belonged or could belong to the people of the United States as a whole. It belonged to the *people*, yes, but to the peoples of the separate *states*. The American people had never been a political entity. "During their colonial condition they formed distinct communities—each with its separate charter and government, and in no way connected with each other, except as dependent members of a common empire." The first effect of the Revolution was to leave the colonies as independent states—independent from one another as well as from the former British government.

"Its next effect was to transfer the sovereignty which had heretofore resided in the British crown, not to the *governments* of, but to the *people* composing the *several* States."

To some it might appear that, in the process of transfer from the British crown to the American states, sovereignty must have been divided and, indeed, divided twice—first, as between Britain and America, and second, as among the thirteen states. But it did not seem so to Calhoun.

After the Declaration of Independence and the extinction of British authority in the colonies, he explained further, nothing remained of the colonial governments except the "popular and representative" branches. "But a representative government, even when entire, cannot possibly be the seat of sovereignty —the supreme and ultimate power of a State. The very term *representative* implies a superior in the individual or body represented." That superior, in the case of the new states, was the body of voters in each of them. "The mere will of the sovereign communities—aided by the remaining fragments, the popular branches of their several colonial governments—speedily ordained and established governments, each for itself." That is, each state adopted a constitution.

Thus commenced the division between the constitution-making and the law-making powers—between the power which ordains and establishes the fundamental laws—which creates, organizes, and invests government with its authority, and subjects it to restrictions—and the power that passes acts to carry into execution the powers thus delegated to the government. The one, emanating from the people as forming a *sovereign community*, creates the government; the other, as a representative appointed to execute its powers, enacts laws to regulate and control the conduct of the people regarded as *individuals*. This division between the two powers—thus necessarily incident to the separation from the parent country—constitutes an element in our political system as essential to its formation as the great and primary territorial division of independent and sovereign States.[19]

This distinction between constitution-making and law-making powers was essential to Calhoun's theory, whether or not it had been essential to the formation of new governments after the break with the mother country.

As a matter of historical fact, the distinction was *not* observed by all the states when they adopted their first constitutions. Jefferson then believed, as Calhoun was later to assert, that the constitutions must come from the people, who should hold special conventions and afterward vote on ratification. Actually, conventions were held in only three states, referendums in only five, and both a convention and a referendum in only one—Massachusetts. In most of the states the *legislatures*, though not elected specifically for that purpose, took it upon themselves to draft new constitutions. In Rhode Island and Connecticut the legislatures merely revised the old colonial charters. Thus, during the Revolution the lawmaking power and the constitution-making power were, in practice, confused.

Nevertheless, Calhoun argued that the people of each state, acting in their sovereign capacity and in a special way, had set up a constitution and, through it, had delegated certain powers to the state government. The same people, acting again in their sovereign capacity, later established a second Constitution and, through this one, delegated certain other powers to the government of the United States. Thereafter the people of each state possessed two governments, and these two, within their respective spheres, were equal and coordinate. Neither was above the other, but the sovereign people of each state were above both. As Calhoun expressed the essential idea:

> Ours is a system of governments, compounded of the separate governments of the several States composing the Union and of one common government of all its members, called the Government of the United States. The former preceded the latter, which was created by their agency. Each was framed by written constitutions; those of the several States by the people of each, acting separately and in their sovereign character; and that of the United States by the same, acting in the same character—but jointly instead of separately.[20]

The sovereign communities, according to Calhoun, delegated only governmental powers and not one bit of their respective sovereignties.

Certainly, as he pointed out, the delegates to the constitutional convention of 1787–88 were elected from the states and voted by states. The document was ratified by conventions within the states. No delegates were elected from the country at large, and neither in drafting nor in ratifying the Constitution did any delegates represent the people as a whole. No nationwide political community created the Constitution. And the Constitution, Calhoun reasoned, created no nationwide political community.

> Laying aside all intermediate agencies, the people of the several States, in their sovereign capacity, agree to unite themselves together in the closest possible connection that could be formed without merging their respective sovereignties into one common sovereignty—to establish one common

government for certain specific objects which, regarding the mutual interest and security of each and all, they supposed could be more certainly, safely, and effectually promoted by it than by their several separate governments.[21]

True, Calhoun conceded, the preamble of the Constitution reads that "We the people of the United States" ordain and establish the new government. But this phrase proves nothing, he said. The term "United States" had been used earlier to designate the thirteen states in Congress assembled, even though the Articles of Confederation specifically recognized the sovereignty of the separate states. Here was a mere problem in semantics, Calhoun thought (though, of course, he did not use that word; it had not yet been invented). The phrase "the people of the United States" could be ambiguous, for it was sometimes used in a territorial or geographical sense. "In this sense, the people of the United States may mean *all* the people living within these limits, without reference to the States or Territories in which they may reside, or of which they may be citizens," Calhoun admitted. But he said the phrase, in its political sense, refers to *"the States united,* which inversion alone, without further explanation, removes the ambiguity." [22] There was, strictly speaking, no United States. There were only the States United.

The Constitution, Calhoun repeated over and over, was a "compact" between the states (that is, between the sovereign communities). By this compact they set up a federal government for common ends. In lawyer's language, the states were the principals, and the federal government was the agent whom they had authorized to act for them. The principals gave specific instructions to the agent in the compact that the principals had made among themselves. That is, they specified the powers and purposes of the federal government in the Constitution. Naturally, according to Calhoun's reasoning, the states themselves must interpret the Constitution and decide when or whether the federal government was exceeding its powers—just as, in law, the principal determines whether his agent is carrying out the instructions given to him. Calhoun wrote:

> Against these conclusive arguments, as they seem to me, it is objected that, if one of the parties has the right to judge of infractions of the Constitution, so has the other; and that, consequently, in cases of contested powers between a State and the General Government, each would have a right to maintain its opinion, as is the case when sovereign powers differ in the construction of treaties or compacts; and that, of course, it would come to be a mere question of force. The error is in the assumption that the General Government is a party to the constitutional compact. The States, as has been shown, formed the compact, acting as sovereign and independent communities. The General Government is but its creature; and though in reality a government, with all the rights and authority which belong to any other government, within the orbit of its powers, it is nevertheless a government emanating from a compact between sovereigns, and partaking, in its nature and object, of the character of a joint commission, appointed to superintend and administer the interests in which all are jointly concerned; but having, beyond its proper sphere, no more power than if it did not exist.[23]

If, in Calhoun's logic, it was erroneous to suppose that the federal government had an equal right to judge, it was of course still more erroneous to suppose that the federal government had an exclusive right to judge. The Supreme Court of the United States was only a branch of the federal government. So the Supreme Court could no more decide constitutional issues involving state powers than an agent or commissioner could decide the intent of the principal who commissioned and instructed him.

Not the Supreme Court but the people of the states must make the decision. "As parties to the constitutional compact, they retain the right, unrestricted, which appertains to such a relation in all cases where it is not surrendered, to judge as to the extent of the obligation imposed by the agreement or compact." But there were a number of states, all sovereign and independent, and no one of them could judge for the others. By what procedure, then, could the states, together, interpret the Constitution?

Calhoun found the answer in the amending process. The states could *interpret* the Constitution in the same way that they could *amend* it—and in essentially the same way that they had used to *ratify* it in the first place. The Constitution prescribes two methods of proposing amendments: by Congress, two-thirds of both houses concurring, or by a special convention called by Congress at the request of two-thirds of the state legislatures. The Constitution also prescribes two methods for ratifying amendments and thus giving them vitality and force. They may be ratified by either state conventions or state legislatures, but, whether through their conventions or through their legislatures, three-fourths of the states must act. In ratifying the Constitution itself, nine of the thirteen states (or approximately three-fourths of them) had been required to approve by means of specially called conventions before the Constitution was to go into effect as among those nine.

Here again the distinction between the constitution-making power and the lawmaking power was not quite as clear-cut as Calhoun assumed. For the Constitution could be made—that is, added to or amended—exclusively by the legislative power of the federal and state governments.

The question remained: how would the amending process be put into operation when needed? Calhoun answered that it was the duty of the federal government, before undertaking to exercise any power not clearly delegated to it in the Constitution, to seek an amendment specifically delegating that power. The burden of proof rested with the federal government, since it, after all, was only an agent of the states. Thus, for example, Congress ought to propose an amendment for a protective tariff and secure approval from three-fourths of the states before attempting to pass any law levying duties for the protection of industry. If, however, Congress failed to secure authorization in advance, and went ahead and passed a law which the people of any state considered unconstitutional, then the people of that state could take steps to protect themselves and at the same time to require an amendment to the Constitution if the law of Congress was to be sustained.

The recourse of the aggrieved state was nullification. For the right of the state, as the principal, to judge the actions of its agent "necessarily involves the right of pronouncing whether an act of the federal government or any of its departments be or be not in conformity to the provisions of the constitutional compact; and, if decided to be inconsistent, of pronouncing it to be unauthorized by the Constitution and therefore null, void, and of no effect," so far as the nullifying state is concerned. This right to nullify was, Calhoun believed, essential if a state was to prevent encroachment upon its "reserved powers"—that is, the powers not delegated in the Constitution but reserved to the states by the Tenth Amendment.

Nullification, as he saw it, was not destructive but constructive. It tended not to disunion but to the maintenance of the Union. It was a "conservative principle." It recreated the Constitution by bringing into play the power that had created it—the ratifying and amending power, consisting of the sovereign communities of three-fourths of the states.

Thus the power which, in its simple and absolute form, was the creator, becomes in its modified form the preserver of the system. By no other device, nor in any other form, could the high functions appertaining to this character be safely and efficiently discharged—and by none other could the system be preserved. It is, when properly understood, the *vis medicatrix* of the system—its great repairing, healing, and conservative power—intended to remedy its disorders, in whatever cause or causes originating, whether in the original errors or defects of the Constitution itself, or the operation of time and change of circumstances, or in conflicts between its parts—including those between the co-ordinate governments. By it alone can the equilibrium of the various powers and divisions of the system be preserved, as by it alone can the stronger be prevented from encroaching on and finally absorbing the weaker. For this purpose it is, as has been shown, entirely safe and all-sufficient. In performing its high functions it acts not as a judicial power but in the far more elevated and authoritative character of an *amending* power—the only one in which it can be called into action at all. In this character it can amend the Constitution by modifying its existing provisions or in case of disputed power—whether it be between the federal government and one of its co-ordinates, or between the former and an interposing State—by declaring, authoritatively, what is the Constitution.[24]

In Calhoun's scheme a state would nullify a federal act—and thus bring the grand amending power into operation—by the action of the sovereign community. That is, the legislature would call a convention, the voters would elect delegates to it, and these representatives of the sovereign community would declare the act null and void. (The legislature itself would not do the nullifying, as Madison and Jefferson had suggested in the Virginia and Kentucky resolutions of 1798–99.) Once the state had passed its ordinance of nullification, the federal law would remain null and void in that state, according to the theory, unless and until three-fourths of the remaining states should approve a constitutional amendment conferring upon the federal government the power to enact the law that had been nullified.

Admittedly, the amending process was rather complex and slow, and it allowed only one more than one-fourth of the states (and conceivably the least populous ones at that) to frustrate the will of all the rest. Calhoun himself calculated (in the 1840's):

As there are at present thirty States in the Union, it will take twenty to propose, and of course would require but eleven to defeat, a proposition to amend the Constitution—or nineteen votes in the Senate, if it should originate in Congress, and the votes of eleven legislatures if it should be to call a convention. By the census of 1840 the federal population of all the States—including the three which were then Territories but which have since become States—was 16,077,604. To this add Texas, since admitted, say 110,000—making the aggregate 16,187,604. Of this amount, the eleven smallest

States (Vermont being the largest of the number) contained a federal population of but 1,638,521; and yet they can prevent the other nineteen States, with a federal population of 14,549,082, from even proposing amendments to the Constitution; while the twenty smallest (of which Maine is the largest), with a federal population of 3,526,811, can compel Congress to call a convention to propose amendments, against the united votes of the other ten, with a federal population of 12,660,793. Thus, while less than one eighth of the population may, in the one case, prevent the adoption of a proposition to amend the Constitution, less than one fourth can, in the other, adopt it.

But striking as are these results, the process, when examined with reference to the ratification of proposals to amend, will present others still more so. Here the consent of three fourths of the States is required—which, with the present number, would make the concurrence of twenty-three States necessary to give effect to the act of ratification and, of course, puts it in the power of any eight States to defeat a proposal to amend. The federal population of the eight smallest is but 776,969; and yet, small as this is, they can prevent amendments against the united votes of the other twenty-two, with a federal population of 15,410,-635, or nearly twenty times their number. But while so small a portion of the entire population can prevent an amendment, twenty-three of the smallest States—with a federal population of only 7,254,400—can amend the Constitution against the united votes of the other seven, with a federal population of 8,933,204. So that a numerical minority of the population can amend the Constitution against a decided numerical majority; when, at the same time, one nineteenth of the population can prevent the other eighteen nineteenths from amending it.[25]

Yet Calhoun felt that the requirements for proposing and ratifying amendments were fair and, indeed, essential. These requirements were enough to prevent the "dominant portion of the Union" from oppressing the weaker portion. They were also sufficient to keep a "combination of a few States" from hindering the rest in making amendments that might be wise and necessary.

Actually, of course, despite his calculations of hypothetical state groupings for and against amendments, Calhoun really was concerned with only one kind of state alignment—that of North and South, free and slave commonwealths. At the time he made his calculations, there were fifteen free and fifteen slave states. If South Carolina, for example, were to nullify a law affecting slavery or some other interest of the South, she could count upon the probability that the rest of the slave states—fourteen of them—would fail to approve an amendment authorizing the nullified law. These other states would not have to act; inaction would suffice. And so, in theory, South Carolina could hardly lose a constitutional test case which she brought about by nullification.

But suppose that, somehow, in an unforeseeable contingency, the nullifying state should be opposed by three-fourths of all the states. Suppose that, with their support, the Constitution were to be amended so as to confer on the federal government the power which the one state had denied. Would that state then have to yield to the rest? Would it have to accept and permit the execution of all federal laws? Not necessarily, according to Calhoun. The state would still have a choice of alternatives. It might give in. Or, in certain circumstances, it might secede.

In the minds of many of Calhoun's contemporaries, Northern as well as Southern, secession could conceivably be justified as a revolutionary right. After all, the thirteen colonies had seceded from the British Empire. The justifying principle was expressed in the Declaration of Independence: governments are instituted among men to secure the rights of life, liberty, and the pursuit of happiness; "whenever any form of government becomes destructive of these ends, it is the right of the people to alter or to abolish it, and to institute a new government." Daniel Webster, for one, upheld the right of revolution, and so did Abraham Lincoln; both men cheered on the Hungarian rebels who were attempting (1848–52) to gain independence from the Ottoman Empire.[26] This sort of right to independence was based, ultimately, on John Locke's theory that men once had lived in a state of nature and had acquired certain natural rights which were anterior to government.

Having repudiated the Lockean assumption of natural rights, Calhoun was estopped from basing upon it his rationalization for secession. But he needed no such assumption. In his opinion, secession was a *constitutional* right. He based it on the same amending or ratifying power on which he based the right of nullification. Each state, in the beginning, had *acceded* to the Union by calling a convention and passing an ordinance of ratification. Any state could *secede* from the Union by calling a convention and repealing the ordinance. Or, for that matter, a state nullifying a federal law could secede simply by refusing to acquiesce in the law after the Constitution had been amended to empower it. Calhoun explained:

But the result is in some respects different where a State, acting in her sovereign character, and as a party to the constitutional compact, has interposed and declared an act of the federal government to be unauthorized by the Constitution and therefore null and void. In this case, if the act of the latter be predicated on a power consistent with the character of the Constitution, the ends for which it was established, and the nature of our system of government—or, more briefly, if it come fairly within the scope of the amending power—the State is bound to acquiesce by the solemn obligation which it contracted in ratifying the Constitution. But if it transcends the limits of the amending power—be inconsistent with the character of the Constitution and with the ends for which it was established, or with the nature of the system—the result is different. In such case, the State is not bound to acquiesce. It may choose whether it will or whether it will not secede from the Union. One or the other course it must take. To refuse acquiescence would be tantamount to secession, and place it as entirely in the relation of a foreign State to the other States as would a positive act of secession. That a State, as a party to the constitutional compact, has the right to secede—acting in the same capacity in which it ratified the Constitution—cannot with any show of reason be denied by any one who regards the Constitution as a compact—if a power should be inserted by the amending power which would radically change the character of the Constitution or the nature of the system, or if the former should fail to fulfil the ends for which it was established. This results, necessarily, from the nature of a compact where the parties to it are sovereign and, of course, have no higher authority to which to appeal. That the effect of secession would be to place her in the relation of a foreign State to the others is equally clear. Nor is it less so that it would make her (not

her citizens *individually*) responsible to them in
that character. All this results, necessarily, from
the nature of a compact between sovereign parties.[27]

According to Calhoun's theory, then, nullification
was possibly though not necessarily a step toward secession. The "concurrent majority" of the aggrieved
state, facing the numerical majority of the States United, would play a game of heads-I-win-and-tails-you-
lose. Having nullified, the state would come out ahead
unless the Constitution were amended, and the odds
were that it would not be, but even if it was, the state
could still have the game by seceding.

STATE POWERS AND SLAVERY

Furthermore, according to Calhoun's theory, nullification was a game that, in the slave controversy, only
one side could play. State interposition to defend slavery was one thing; state interposition to protect the
slave was quite another, and it was forbidden by Calhoun's rules.

Most of the Northern states tried their own brand of
nullification after the decision of the United States Supreme Court in the case of *Prigg* v. *the Commonwealth
of Pennsylvania* (1842). In that case the Supreme
Court held that the return of fugitive slaves, in accord-
ance with the fugitive-slave law of 1793, was a federal
and not a state responsibility. Thereafter all but one or
two of the Northern states adopted "personal-liberty"
laws, which hindered the enforcement of the fugitive-
slave law by forbidding state officials to aid in the arrest of fugitives, denying the use of state jails for the
detention of captives, and requiring jury trials for al-
leged slaves who claimed to be free. Calhoun did not

like that kind of nullification. By such "hostile acts," he complained, not only federal law but a constitutional provision was "evaded and, in effect, annulled." [28]

There is no reason to suppose that Calhoun would have liked it any better if the Northern states, in annulling the fugitive-slave law, had followed his own procedure by calling conventions and adopting nullification ordinances. For, to him, the South's "peculiar institution" was indeed peculiar. Slavery occupied a special place in American life and in the Constitution itself.

Logically, Calhoun justified slavery by his assumption of human inequality as necessary and desirable in all civilized societies (though psychologically it no doubt was the reverse: he assumed the necessity and desirability of human inequality in order to justify slavery). He did more than merely justify the institution: he praised it as "a good—a positive good." It was good for nonslaveholders, North as well as South; their prosperity depended upon it. It was good for the slaves themselves. It fed, sheltered, and clothed them better and made them healthier and happier than free Negroes or even wage-earning whites.

Regardless of its positive virtues, slavery was, according to Calhoun, the only arrangement by which two races so different as the white and the black could live together in progress and peace. Its abolition could not make true freemen out of Negroes: they were naturally inferior, naturally slaves, and if they ceased to be the slaves of individual masters, they would become the slaves of the community as a whole. Or, with the power of the federal government behind them, Southern Negroes would become the *masters,* and Southern whites the slaves! Calhoun warned:

To destroy the existing relation between the free and servile races at the South would lead to consequences unparalleled in history. They cannot be separated, and cannot live together in peace or harmony or to their mutual advantage except in their present relation. Under any other, wretchedness and misery and desolation would overspread the whole South. The example of the British West Indies, as blighting as emancipation has proved to them, furnishes a very faint picture of the calamities it would bring on the South. . . .

Very different would be the circumstances under which emancipation would take place with us. If it ever should be effected, it would be through the agency of the Federal Government, controlled by the dominant power of the Northern States of the Confederacy, against the resistance and struggle of the Southern. It can then only be effected by the prostration of the white race; and that would necessarily engender the bitterest feelings of hostility between them and the North. But the reverse would be the case between the blacks of the South and the people of the North. Owing their emancipation to them, they [the blacks] would regard them as friends, guardians, and patrons, and centre, accordingly, all their sympathy in them. The people of the North would not fail to reciprocate and to favor them, instead of the whites. Under the influence of such feelings, and impelled by fanaticism and love of power, they [the Northerners] would not stop at emancipation. Another step would be taken—to raise them [the freed slaves] to a political and social equality with their former owners by giving them the right of voting and holding public offices under the Federal Government. . . . But when once raised to an equality, they would become the fast political associates of the North, acting and voting with them on all questions, and by this political union between them, holding the white race at the South in complete subjection. The blacks and the profligate whites that might unite with them would become the principal recipients of federal offices and patronage and would, in consequence, be raised above the whites of the South in the political and social scale. We would, in a word, change conditions with them—a degradation greater than has ever yet fallen to the lot of a free and enlightened people, and one from which we could not escape, should emancipation take place (which it certainly will if not prevented), but by fleeing the homes of ourselves and ancestors and by abandoning our country to our former slaves, to become the permanent abode of disorder, anarchy, poverty, misery, and wretchedness.[29]

Thus, in 1849, Calhoun prophesied accurately (as white Southerners later were to view it) what was to befall the South in less than twenty years.

In Calhoun's opinion, abolitionism was a "disease of the body politic," and a very dangerous disease. The abolitionists, he conceded, did not pretend that the federal government had the power, constitutionally, to emancipate the slaves within the Southern states. But the abolitionists, together with a growing number of sympathizers in the North, did claim that the federal government had the power, constitutionally, to abolish slavery in the District of Columbia and other places under federal jurisdiction, to exclude it from the territories, and to prohibit the interstate slave trade. If the federal government should adopt such measures as these, Calhoun believed, they would lead surely to complete emancipation—"and that at no distant day." He explained:

Little, in truth, would be left to be done after we

have been excluded from all the territories, including those to be hereafter acquired; after slavery is abolished in this District and in the numerous places dispersed all over the South where Congress has the exclusive right of legislation, and after the other measures proposed are consummated. Every outpost and barrier would be carried, and nothing would be left but to finish the work of abolition at pleasure in the States themselves. This District and all places over which Congress has exclusive power of legislation would be asylumn for fugitive slaves, where, as soon as they placed their feet, they would become, according to the doctrines of our Northern assailants, free, unless there should be some positive enactments to prevent it.

Under such a state of things the probability is that emancipation would soon follow, without any final act to abolish slavery. The depressing effects of such measures on the white race at the South, and the hope they would create in the black of a speedy emancipation, would produce a state of feeling inconsistent with the much longer continuance of the existing relations between the two. . . . To these may be added an aggression, though not yet commenced, long meditated and threatened: to prohibit what the abolitionists call the internal slave trade, meaning thereby the transfer of slaves from one State to another, from whatever motive done, or however effected. Their object would seem to be to render them worthless by crowding them together where they are, and thus hasten the work of emancipation. . . .

But . . . if the calculations of policy should retard the adoption of these measures, or even defeat them altogether, there would be still left one certain way to accomplish their object, if the determination avowed by the North to monopolize all

the territories, to the exclusion of the South,
should be carried into effect. That of itself would,
at no distant day, add to the North a sufficient
number of States to give her three fourths of the
whole; when, under the color of an amendment of
the Constitution, she would emancipate our slaves,
however opposed it [the amendment] might be to
its [the Constitution's] true intent.[30]

So far as Calhoun was concerned, nullification was a
constitutional device by which a slave state might resist that kind of legislation, and secession was a constitutional device by which a slave state might escape
that kind of amendment. *His* system of state interposition followed from the nature and spirit of the Constitution itself; the "hostile acts" of the Northern legislatures did not. For the "true intent" of the Constitution
was to protect slavery and guarantee its continued existence.

Slavery, Calhoun argued, was a key item in the constitutional compact. "It is the only property recognized
by it," he wrote; "the only one that entered into its formation as a political element, both in the adjustment of
the relative weight of the States in the Government,
and the apportionment of direct taxes; and the only one
that is put under the express guaranty of the Constitution." Here he had in mind the three-fifths compromise,
by which three-fifths of the slaves were to be counted
in deciding how many representatives a state should
have in Congress and how large a share of direct taxes
(if any such taxes were levied) it should pay. He also
had in mind the provision for the return, from one state
to another, of fugitives from labor or service—the provision on which the fugitive-slave law of 1793 had been
based.

This provision, he suggested, was part of an "understanding" between the constitutional convention and

the old Confederation Congress. In the summer of 1787, while the convention was providing for the return of fugitives, the Congress passed the Northwest Ordinance, with its prohibition of slavery in the Northwest Territory. "It is probable that there was an understanding," Calhoun imagined, ". . . as the old Congress and the convention were then in session in the same place." [31]

The sovereign communities of the slave states, he insisted, agreed to the constitutional compact only because it guaranteed slavery. Hence it was unconstitutional, at least in spirit, for any Northern state even to permit antislavery agitation, to say nothing of passing a personal-liberty law. Calhoun felt outraged when, in 1835, none of the Northern legislatures complied with the request from various Southern legislatures that the circulation of "incendiary" literature be stopped.

Certainly, in his view, the federal government had an obligation to promote slavery interests to the fullest extent of its delegated powers. One of these was the conduct of foreign affairs. In his reply (1844) to the British minister, in which he justified Texas annexation as a means of protecting slavery, Calhoun explained that some of the American states maintained the institution, and others did not.

With us it is a question to be decided not by the Federal Government but by each member of this Union, for itself, according to its own views of domestic policy, and without any right on the part of the Federal Government to interfere in any manner whatever. Its rights and duties are limited to protecting, under the guarantees of the Constitution, each member of this Union, in whatever policy it may adopt in reference to that portion within its respective limits.

As the "common representative and protector" of all the states, the American government had an "imperious duty" to thwart British diplomacy with regard to Texas.[32] In other words, the Constitution enjoined upon the United States a proslavery foreign policy.

The Constitution also required proslavery domestic policies, so far as federal jurisdiction went. In carrying the mails, in governing the District of Columbia, in regulating interstate commerce, in legislating for the territories—in exercising any of its powers—the government could act only as an agent or "trustee" for the sovereign communities that had created it. It must not discriminate against any of them or their property. Some, who held property in slaves, had agreed to the arrangement, in the first place, only on condition that this species of property be specially guaranteed. So, by Calhoun's logic, the United States government was preeminently an agency for the protection of slavery.

Calhoun developed his theory of the "trust powers" of the federal government most fully in the course of his argument (1848) that neither Congress nor the people of the territories could constitutionally exclude slavery from them. Speaking on the bill for the organization of Oregon territory, he began by saying:

> There is a very striking difference between the position on which the slaveholding and non-slaveholding States stand, in reference to the subject under consideration. The former desire no action of the Government; demand no law to give them any advantage in the territory about to be established; are willing to leave it, and other territories belonging to the United States, open to all their citizens, so long as they continue to be territories —and when they cease to be so, to leave it to their inhabitants to form such governments as

may suit them, without restriction or condition,
except that imposed by the Constitution, as a prerequisite for admission into the Union. In short,
they are willing to leave the whole subject where
the Constitution and the great and fundamental
principles of self-government place it. On the contrary, the non-slaveholding States, instead of being
willing to leave it on this broad and equal foundation, demand the interposition of the Government
and the passage of an act to prevent the citizens
of the slaveholding States from emigrating with
their property into the territory, in order to give
their citizens and those they may permit, the exclusive right of settling it, while it remains in that
condition, preparatory to subjecting it to like restrictions and conditions when it becomes a State.

Northern free-soilers contended that Congress had the
absolute right to govern a territory. They quoted the
Constitution: "Congress shall have power to dispose
of and make all needful rules and regulations respect-
ing the territory and other property belonging to the
United States." But Calhoun denied that these words
conferred "any governmental power whatever" upon
Congress. They referred only to territory "regarded as
public lands," that is, as real estate. True, Congress
had the *exclusive* power with regard to the territories,
but only the power to make necessary rules and regulations—quite a different thing from *legislative* or governmental power. Certainly, Congress had no *absolute*
power over the territories or any other subject. The
power of Congress was subject to important restrictions.

I refer to those imposed on the trustees by the
nature and character of the party who constituted
the trustees and invested them with the trust pow-

ers to be exercised for its benefit. In this case it is the United States, that is, the several States of the Union. It was they who constituted the Government as their representative or trustee and intrusted it with powers to be exercised for their common and joint benefit. To them in their united character the territories belong, as is expressly declared by the Constitution. They are the joint and common owners [of the territories], regarded as property or land; and in them, severally, reside the dominion or sovereignty over them. They are as much the territories of one State as another —of Virginia as of New York, of the Southern as the Northern States. They are the territories of all, because they are the territories of each; and not of each, because they are the territories of the whole. Add to this the perfect equality of dignity, as well as of rights, which appertain to them as members of a common federal Union—which all writers on the subject admit to be a fundamental and essential relation between States so united— and it must be manifest that Congress, in governing the territories, can give no preference or advantage to one State over another, or to one portion or section of the Union over another, without depriving the State or section over which the preference is given, or from which the advantage is withheld, of their clear and unquestionable right, and subverting the very foundation on which the Union and Government rest. It has no more power to do so than to subvert the Constitution itself.

Hence Congress could not rightfully keep Southerners from migrating to any territory with their slaves, nor could the inhabitants or the legislatures of the territory do so. To suppose that the inhabitants or the legislatures had the power would be absurd. "The first half-dozen of squatters would become the sovereigns . . . and the conquered people of New Mexico and California would become the sovereigns . . . vested with the full right of excluding even their conquerors." But the people of the United States already were the sovereigns, and sovereignty could not be divided.[33]

Thus the Calhoun doctrine emphasized state *powers* as well as state *rights*. The powers of the slave states extended beyond the state boundaries. These powers reached into the territories, where Congress, with no legislative discrimination of its own, must simply recognize and give effect to the state laws—that is, the laws that created property in slaves. These powers reached into the free states themselves, to the extent that those states were obligated to return fugitives and to suppress antislavery activity. These powers reached even beyond the borders of the United States, into the Republic of Texas, for example, where the federal government was required to use its diplomatic functions in order to forestall abolition.

The Calhoun doctrine was not, as it might seem at first glance, simply a doctrine of local self-determination, of state defense against aggression from without. True, Calhoun accused the North of agggression, but only in the territories, the District, or other areas outside the Southern states. By his reasoning, slavery was national, freedom was local, and slaveholders had rights that antislavery men were bound to respect, but not the other way around.

THE CLASS STRUGGLE

As a spokesman for the Southern planters, who were being more and more reduced to a minority status in the country as a whole, Calhoun increasingly emphasized the conflict between the North and the South, the nonslaveholding and the slaveholding states. For him, the term "numerical majority" most of the time meant the population of the North. Yet his theory of the concurrent majority recognized the possibility of conflict among interest groups of various kinds. He never listed these at length, never gave much specific content to his concept of "interests." Yet, in addition to "the North" and "the South," he did mention "capital" and "labor" as antagonistic elements, and sometimes he used the term "numerical majority" in referring to the working class. Indeed, he spoke again and again of the capital-and-labor conflict, and this theme had a crucial role in his thinking, though events compelled him to subordinate it to the slavery-and-abolition conflict. Unless this theme is taken into account, his theory of the concurrent majority, with its corollary of nullification, cannot be fully appreciated.[34]

Before Calhoun, other American thinkers had given a place in their thinking to the class struggle as an actuality or a potentiality. The idea was familiar enough to a generation of Americans brought up largely on the history of ancient Greece and Rome. Calhoun, however, developed the idea much further than his American predecessors (or, for that matter, his European predecessors) had done. In his approach to the subject he anticipated Karl Marx and Friedrich Engels, the founders of "scientific" socialism, though in spirit, purpose, and conclusion he differed utterly from them.

He started, as Marx and Engels also were to do, with John Locke's labor theory of value. From that assumption he deduced that in all societies of the past and present, except the most primitive, there existed a system of exploitation of a working class. "Let those who are interested remember," he once said, "that labor is the only source of wealth, and how small a portion of it, in all old and civilized countries, even the best governed, is left to those by whose labor wealth is created." [35] On another occasion he repeated that "there never has yet existed a wealthy and civilized society in which one portion of the community did not, in point of fact, live on the labor of the other," and that "it would not be difficult to trace the various devices by which the wealth of all civilized communities has been so unequally divided, and to show by what means so small a share has been allocated to those by whose labor it was produced, and so large a share given to the nonproducing classes." [36]

In his references to the capitalistic producing and nonproducing groups Calhoun used terms that were neither consistent nor precise. He spoke of "labor" and "capital," "the poor" and "the rich," "the operatives" and "the capitalists," "the ignorant and dependent" and "the intelligence of the community," "the needy and corrupt" and "the wealthy and talented," and so forth. The terms themselves indicated where his own sympathies lay, and yet he declared, at a time (1842) when he was looking to the presidency and hoping for the labor vote: "No one is more averse to the reduction of wages than I am, or entertains a greater respect for the laboring portion of the community." [37]

Calhoun anticipated a number of other Marxist doctrines, besides the idea of labor exploitation. Among these were the following: (1) the eventual division of society into only two classes, capitalist and proletarian; (2) the gradual expropriation of most of the population by the capitalists, so that the propertied would become fewer and fewer and the propertyless more and more numerous; and (3) the ultimate impoverishment of the masses to a bare-subsistence level.

All this, Calhoun thought, would come about through the use of governmental powers for the benefit of the capitalists. In private conversation he once talked of "capital and operatives." His hearer recorded that he

> spoke of the tendency of Capital to destroy and
> absorb the property of society and produce a col-
> lision between itself and operatives. The Federal
> Govt. by its distribution of revenues creates capi-
> talists, and operates upon the labour of the States.
> Took the instance of 100 men without a Govt. and
> showed the equilibrium that would prevail. Sup-
> posed a Government that would give $5000 to ten
> of the hundred and then traced the tendency of
> the Capital to eradicate the possession of the soil,
> and to reduce the 90 to a state of simple opera-
> tives.[38]

There were various fiscal means by which a government might present a bounty to a favored group and
thus enable it to expropriate the rest of society, but
the most important of these devices, in Calhoun's
belief, was the protective tariff. Such governmental
"intermeddling" in economic affairs, in Europe, had
brought about an "unequal and unjust distribution of
wealth between the several classes or portions of the
community."

In the United States the first effect of the tariff had
been to enrich the North and impoverish the South,
but the time would come when it would redistribute
property as between social classes rather than geographical sections. Calhoun predicted:

> After we [the planters] are exhausted, the contest
> will be between the capitalists and operatives; for
> into these two classes it must, ultimately, divide
> society. The issue of the struggle here must be
> the same as it has been in Europe. Under the
> operation of the [protective] system, wages must

sink more rapidly than the prices of the necessaries of life, till the operatives will be reduced to the lowest point—when the portion of the products of their labor left to them will be barely sufficient to preserve existence.[39]

In consequence of the exploitation and expropriation of the working class, according to Calhoun as later according to Marx, class conflict inevitably would arise. As the conditions producing it became more and more extreme, the conflict would grow increasingly intense. Finally it would culminate in a revolutionary crisis.

"It is useless to disguise the fact," Calhoun frankly informed his fellow senators (1837). "There is and always has been, in an advanced stage of wealth and civilization, a conflict between capital and labor."[40] This "tendency to conflict in the North," he said at another time, "is constantly on the increase."[41] And again: "Where wages command labor, as in the non-slaveholding States, there necessarily takes place between labor and capital a conflict which leads, in process of time, to disorder, anarchy, and revolution, if not counteracted by some appropriate and strong constitutional provision."

For, as the community becomes populous, wealthy, refined, and highly civilized, the difference between the rich and the poor will become more strongly marked; and the number of the ignorant and dependent greater in proportion to the rest of the community. With the increase of this difference, the tendency to conflict between them will become stronger; and, as the poor and dependent become more numerous in proportion, there will be . . . no want of leaders among the wealthy and ambitious, to excite and direct them in their efforts to obtain the control.[42]

Here Calhoun doubtless had in mind the history of the Greek city-states and the Roman republic, where leaders from the upper class often led the lower class in its revolutionary effort. Still, he was predicting, as Marx and Engels also were to do, that leaders would defect from the bourgeoisie to aid the proletariat in its forthcoming struggle.

In his political prognoses Calhoun displayed a fairly definite notion of historical determinism, with similarities to the later Marxist dialectical materialism. As he watched "the unfolding of the great events" of the European revolutionary movements of 1848, he was confident he could foretell the outcome, for he had the benefit of principles "drawn from facts in the moral world just as certain as any in the physical." He insisted "it ought never to be forgotten that *the past is the parent of the present*" (he underlined the words). But he did not believe the historical process was necessarily one of continuous growth. A society might contain the seeds of its own destruction. Thus "the past condition of Europe," though it had "given birth" to the most advanced civilization hitherto known, might have, "indeed, contained within itself causes calculated to retard or prevent a further progress." The continued advance of material improvement, growing out of the many inventions and discoveries over the past century, could be expected only if the changes in means and methods of production and distribution should be accompanied by suitable changes in the organization of society and government.

"What I dread," wrote Calhoun, expressing his own concept of cultural lag, "is that progress in political science falls far short of progress in that which relates to matter, and which may lead to convulsions and rev-

olutions that may retard or even arrest the former." [43]
He was more optimistic when he took a long-run view.
The many discoveries and inventions, particularly "the
application of steam to machinery of almost every
description," though it would "cause changes, political
and social, difficult to be anticipated," must in the end
accrue to the good of mankind.

> It is, however, not improbable that many and
> great but temporary evils will follow the changes
> they have effected and are destined to effect. It
> seems to be a law in the political as well as in the
> material world that great changes cannot be made,
> except very gradually, without convulsions and
> revolutions, to be followed by calamities, in the
> beginning—however beneficial they may prove to
> be in the end. The first effect of such changes, on
> long established governments, will be to unsettle
> the opinions and principles in which they origi-
> nated—and which have guided their policy—be-
> fore those which the changes are calculated to
> form and establish are fairly developed and under-
> stood. The interval between the decay of the old
> and the formation and establishment of the new
> constitutes a period of transition, which must al-
> ways necessarily be one of uncertainty, confusion,
> error, and wild and fierce fanaticism. [44]

Among the "erroneous opinions" that would disturb
the transitional period, much the most serious was the
belief in rule by the "numerical majority," a belief
based upon the "false conception" that men once had
lived in a state of nature and therefore could claim
liberty and equality as natural rights. This error was
"upheaving Europe" in 1848. From the European experience, the falsity of the democratic dogma would

soon become apparent, for, according to Calhoun's dialectic, an everextension of liberty must lead to "a contraction instead of an enlargement of its sphere." Unlimited democracy would be followed by anarchy, and then an "appeal to force," and finally dictatorship, "monarchy in its absolute form." [45] Sooner or later, a similar or worse result, including civil war, must follow for the United States.

But Calhoun saw a way out, for both the United States and Europe. Out of the contradictions in society that gave rise to chaos, an entirely different synthesis might emerge through the application of political science. And by "political science" he meant of course his theory of the concurrent majority, with all its paraphernalia, including some scheme of federation and of "interposition" by the member states, that is, nullification or its equivalent. Thus, as he conceived it, his system was not only a means of protecting slaveowners against abolitionists or planters against capitalists; it was also a way of defending both planters and capitalists against the rising proletarians. He was and is recognized as a champion of the plantation interest, but in his own mind he was more than that: he aspired to lead the combined conservatism of North and South against the universal forces of revolt.

Abolitionism and socialism he viewed as twin attacks upon property, as double dangers arising from the same source, namely, the idea that men are born free and equal. In opposing the reception of abolitionist petitions by the Senate, he said (1836):

The sober and considerate portions of citizens of the non-slaveholding States, who have a deep stake in the existing institutions of the country, would have little forecast not to see that the assaults which are now directed against the institutions of the Southern States may be very easily directed against those which uphold their own property and security. A very slight modification of the arguments used against the institutions which sustain the property and security of the South would make them equally effectual against the institutions of the North, including banking, in which so vast an amount of its property and capital is invested.[46]

So, Calhoun urged, the planters and the capitalists had a common interest in stamping out antislavery propaganda.

For yet another reason they had a common interest in the preservation of slavery, according to Calhoun. The conflict between capital and labor had no place in the Southern way of life. The Southern slave was not so ruthlessly exploited as the Northern or the European wage earner. Consider the various means by which the laborer, slave or free, has been deprived of the fruits of his labor:

The devices are almost innumerable, from the brute force and gross superstition of ancient times to the subtle and artful fiscal contrivances of modern. I might well challenge a comparison between them and the more direct, simple, and patriarchal mode by which the labor of the African race is, among us, commanded by the European [that is, the American]. I may say with truth that in few countries is so much left to the share of the laborer and so little exacted from him or . . . more kind attention paid to him in sickness or infirmities of age. Compare his condition with the tenants of the poor houses in the more civilized portions of Europe—look at the sick and the old or infirm slave, on the one hand, in the midst of his family and friends, under the kind superintending care of his master and mistress, and compare it with the forlorn and wretched condition of the pauper in the poor house. But I will not dwell on this aspect of the question; I turn to the political; and here I fearlessly assert that the existing relation between the two races in the South, against which these blind, fanatics are waging war, forms the most solid and durable foundation on which to rear free and stable political institutions.

The foundations were solid and durable because, on the plantation, there was no division and no conflict between capital and labor. "The Southern States are an aggregate, in fact, of communities, not of individuals. Every plantation is a little community, with the master at its head, who concentrates in himself the united interests of capital and labor, of which he is the common representative." So, on the plantation, capital and labor were "identified," that is, identical. "The blessing of this state of things extends beyond the limits of the South," Calhoun reasoned. "It makes that section the balancer of the [constitutional] system; the great conservative power, which prevents other portions, less fortunately constituted, from rushing into conflict." [47]

Therefore the property owners of the North should not oppose the extension of slavery into the West; they ought to realize that they had as much to gain as the slaveowners themselves in preserving an "equilibrium" of slave and free states.

I was, in this connection, much struck many years ago by a remark made by one of four young English gentlemen, who in passing through this city [Washington] spent some evenings with me—of whom Lord Stanley was one. We were conversing about the causes which, for so long a time, had kept this Union together in peace and harmony. It was regarded as a wonderful phenomenon that a country of such vast extent and of such numerous population should have passed through so many years under free and popular institutions without convulsion or shock. Lord Stanley—without any suggestion or leading remark of mine—said that it was owing to the Southern States, and that it was their conservative tendency that preserved us from disorder. Let gentlemen then be warned that while warring on us they are warring on themselves.[48]

And if the quarrel over the territories should end in disunion, the Northerners and not the Southerners ought to reckon the cost of that event. If left to itself, the North would run the risk of disruption from within, but slavery would save the South.

> From the conservative character of the institution, it would prevent that conflict between labor and capital, which must ever exist in populous and crowded communities, where wages are the regulator between them—and thereby secure and preserve with us a settled and quiet condition of things within, which can never be experienced in such communities. The North, on the contrary, would have no central point of union to bind its various and conflicting interests together; and would, with the increase of its population and wealth, be subject to all the agitation and conflicts growing out of the divisions of wealth and poverty and their concomitants, capital and labor, of which already there are so many and so serious.[49]

In short, the loss of the South to the Union or the

elimination of slavery in the South would open the way for social revolution in the North.

Not only American capitalists but also the British ruling classes had a stake in the preservation of slavery. According to Calhoun's logic, there was no real difference between the subjection of one man to another, as in the South, and the subjection of one class to another, as in the British Isles, or the subjection of one nation to another, as in the British Empire. Hence, in encouraging abolition, the rulers of the Empire were attacking the very principle upon which their own position rested, and were giving rise to such "convulsive" movements as chartism in England and socialism in France.[50]

Calhoun was heard to say that the "interests of the *gentlemen* of the North and of the South" were "identical." He insisted that he was not opposed to capitalism or to capitalists: he was "no enemy of manufactures or of manufacturers, but quite the reverse." He thought the quarrels between planter and capitalist had no such deep and ineradicable causes as the conflict between capitalist and worker. He said that abolitionism originated in no "hostility of interests" between Southerners and Northerners. "The labor of our slaves does not conflict with the profit of their capitalists or the wages of their operatives." Abolitionism originated in "fanaticism," nothing more.[51]

True, the cotton grower and the cotton manufacturer differed on matters like the protective tariff. But this would no longer remain a barrier between them once the tariff question was rightly understood. Calhoun would advise the manufacturers—"if they would hear the voice of one who has ever wished them well"—that the domestic market was entirely "too scanty" for their resources and their skill. They ought to abandon the protective system, which limited exports in proportion as it checked imports, and ought to "march forth fearlessly to meet the world in competition." Once they had "commanded" the foreign market, "all conflict between the planter and the manufacturer would cease." [52] Upon such a policy of commercial imperialism, with cotton going out of the country not as raw stuff but as yarn and fabric, millowners and plantation proprietors might unite in mutual prosperity. Thus nullification, if Northern businessmen would but accept the principle of the concurrent majority, would save them from themselves by setting aside such unwise and uneconomic legislation as the protective tariff.

The principle would be of advantage to Northern businessmen in other ways as well. For one thing, it would enable them to ride the democratic wave without drowning. They could let their employees vote while themselves keeping the upper hand in politics. Suffrage could not safely be extended in governments of the numerical majority, Calhoun explained, "without placing them ultimately under the control of the more ignorant and dependent portions of the community." The case would be different in governments of the concurrent majority. "There, mere numbers have not the absolute control; and the wealthy and intelligent, being identified in interest with the poor and ignorant of their respective portions or interests of the community, become their leaders and protectors." That is to say, the principle of the concurrent majority would have the direct consequence of lessening and limiting the class struggle within a particular area of the country. This principle would tend to "unite the community, let its interests be ever so diversified or opposed." The numerical principle, on the other hand, would tend to "divide it into two conflicting portions, let its interests be, naturally, ever so united and identified." [53] And ultimately the masses, unrestrained by either sentimental or constitutional checks, would overwhelm the "wealthy and intelligent" at the polls. This danger the Calhoun system would forestall.

His system would benefit the property owners of the North in still another way. It would make them and the slaveowners more regardful of one another's interests. The very requirement of unanimity would cause the leaders on both sides to be more conciliatory. As between the gentlemen of the North and the South it would create union and strength, not division and weakness. It would enable them to act together harmoniously in the face of the danger that threatened them both—the danger of a proletarian uprising. Here, as Calhoun put it, was a "common constitutional ground, on which the reflecting and patriotic, of every quarter of the Union, might rally to arrest the approaching catastrophe." [54]

On behalf of the planter class he appealed again and again to fellow conservatives among the bankers and merchants and manufacturers of the North. As each great sectional issue came to a head between 1828 and 1850, he was ready with a new installment of his class-struggle argument. He made the first statement of his thesis in the famous "South Carolina Exposition" itself, in which he denounced the Tariff of 1828 and proposed his nullification procedure as a remedy for the South, but in which he also warned that protectionism would ruin the planter class and leave Northern employers to fight alone the coming battle with their employees. In 1834, when the bank issue was intensified by a sharp financial crisis, he took occasion to point out that a banking system with power to swell and shrink the money supply was as dangerous as the protective system in causing an improper distribution of income and hastening the day of revolution.[55] In 1841 he criticized Henry Clay's distribution bill (for dividing among the several states the proceeds from the sale of public lands) by asserting

[99]

that one of its effects would be to array "one class against another." [56] And during the Mexican War he took his stand against the annexation of *all* of Mexico (large areas of which were unsuited to slavery) on the ground that the creation of an American empire would lead to dangerous social changes within the older Union.[57]

Calhoun did not intend his theory merely as a bogey with which to frighten Northern property owners into yielding on the sectional issues of the day. Nor did he suppose that his words, in themselves, would induce the Northerners to see the light. "That any force of argument can change public opinion," he wrote in 1831, "I do not expect; but I feel assured that the coming confusion and danger, which I have long foreseen, will." [58] Though the revolutionary movements then under way in Europe failed to have the repercussions that he anticipated for the United States, the time of confusion and danger seemed finally at hand when the financial crisis of 1834 hit the nation. Now, Calhoun persuaded himself, his doctrines gained adherents among the well-to-do in the North. Thousands of them looked to the South for protection against the "needy and corrupt" of their own section. "They begin to feel," Calhoun congratulated himself, "that they have more to fear from their own people than we from our slaves." [59] A year later, though the financial crisis had passed without fulfilling his expectations, he still nourished a hope that the capitalists would be converted sooner or later through fear of a mass uprising. He thought:

The first victims would be the wealthy and talented of the North. The intelligence of the North must see this, but whether in time to save themselves and the institutions of the country God only knows. But whenever their eyes may open, they will be astonished to find that the doctrines which they denounced as treason are the only means of their political salvation, while those which they so fondly hugged to their bosom were working their certain destruction.[60]

In 1848, when Calhoun was completing his *Disquisition on Government,* he similarly felt that he could win Northern converts only after the "failure and embarrassment of the French experiment" should have "prepared" the "publick mind" by putting the capitalists in a receptive mood.[61] Not his persuasions, then, but a crisis in the class struggle itself would bring the Northern capitalists into a full alliance with the Southern planters.

Thus Calhoun supposed that the decisive clash between worker and capitalist would appear before the decisive clash between capitalist and planter. Indeed, the one would obviate the other. This order of events was to be reversed in Marxian theory, which holds that the crisis between bourgeoisie and landed aristocracy precedes the crisis between proletariat and bourgeoisie. Calhoun's order of events was also to be reversed in American history: the Civil War was to pit planter and capitalist against one another whereas, if his anticipations had been met, the planter and the capitalist would have fought together against a common foe.

Calhoun's appeal to the Northern capitalist before the Civil War was much like Marx's appeal to the Northern workingman after the war had begun. Both Calhoun and Marx contended, in effect, that the destruction of capitalism would come only after the destruction of the slave economy. Marx, the great revolutionary, itched to see the destruction of both. But Calhoun, the great reactionary, wished to prevent the destruction of either. To the last, while helping to create a sectional patriotism in the South, he persisted in believing it would be impossible for labor and capital to achieve a similar unity in the North. To the last he persisted in hoping that the men of business, increasingly harassed by labor troubles and radical politics, would eventually be only too glad to meet the planters on the planters' terms.

SUMMARY

Calhoun's theory of government, together with its application to the United States of his time, may be summarized as follows:

Human nature is the starting point for governmental theory. Human beings are alike in having both individual (selfish) and social (unselfish) feelings, the former strong, the latter weak. In other respects, however, human beings are not alike. Certainly they are not equal except in a limited, legal sense; they are endowed with widely varying capacities for self-development. Their nature is such that, with insignificant exceptions, they can live only in society and under government.

Government must be strong enough to protect the people not only from outside enemies but also from one another, for their self-interest leads to continual conflicts between individuals and between groups. Yet the people must be allowed the greatest possible liberty, so that they may realize to the fullest their individual potentialities. Since these potentialities vary, the more liberty there is, the more inequality there will be, which is desirable and, indeed, essential for progress. Thus liberty and equality do *not* go together. The proper balancing of security and liberty—or, in other words, of power and liberty—is the central problem of government. Imbalance usually comes from too much power rather than too little; for, like all human beings, rulers, even elected ones, are prone to self-aggrandizement.

A *constitution* is the governmental arrangement by which rulers are checked and power is limited. To be effective, the constitution must pit power against power—negative against positive. The right to vote is essential to constitutional government, but the right to vote is, by itself, insufficient. It results in rule by the numerical majority, that is, rule by the largest group or combination of groups. The rest, the minority or minorities, remain unprotected. They, too, must be provided with a negative power if there is to be a truly limited or constitutional government.

The *concurrent majority*, in addition to the numerical majority, must have a voice. The concurrent majority is the majority of every important group (or interest) taken separately. Under a true constitution, governmental action requires the approval of all the separate majorities as well as the approval of a majority of the people as a whole. Each group, then, must have a veto on governmental action.

Nullification, or state interposition, is, in the United States, a device for providing such a veto. (Nullification thus assumes that important interests are more or less identified with various states, and certainly the slaveholding interest is important to each of the slave states.) Through a special convention, the people of a state can nullify a federal law which they deem unconstitutional. In that state the law then becomes null and void. It remains so unless and until three-fourths of the states ratify a constitutional amendment specifically authorizing the nullified law.

Secession is a possible recourse on the part of the people of the nullifying state if, in their judgment, the new amendment is itself unconstitutional, that is, inconsistent with the original purpose and spirit of the Constitution. The rights of nullification and secession follow inevitably from the nature of sovereignty and of the constitutional compact.

Sovereignty, the ultimate and supreme power within a body politic, is not to be confused with governmental powers. The one is the source for the others. Governmental powers, which are derived from sovereignty, may be delegated and divided; sovereignty itself cannot be. In the United States, sovereignty resides in the people of each of the separate states.

The *constitutional compact* (the American Constitution) is an agreement among the several states as sovereign communities. It is, in effect, the set of instructions which these communities, as the principals, have given to the federal government as their agent or trustee. By the agreement they have delegated certain specified powers but have yielded no sovereignty. The people of each state must decide for themselves whether, in any of its actions, the federal government is exceeding its delegated powers. If the people of one state disagree with those of other states, with regard to the interpretation of the compact, the difference of opinion can be resolved by the amending process. By this process, the federal government is decisively adjudged to have exceeded its powers if one more than one-fourth of all the states agree that it has done so.

Slavery occupies a special place in the constitutional compact. A number of the sovereign communities would never have agreed to the compact without guarantees for slavery. These guarantees form part of the bargain. So far as its legitimate powers go, the federal government, as a trustee for the states, must protect and promote the interests of all of them—and especially the interests of slavery, since human chattels are the only kind of property specifically mentioned in the compact. In the conduct of foreign affairs, in the regulation of interstate commerce, in the management of federal property, in the making of rules for the territories, the federal government cannot use its own discretion but must merely give effect to state laws creating property in slaves.

The *class struggle* is the most serious and most important of all the group conflicts in civilized societies. This struggle arises from the fact that, in all such societies, one class exploits another. In the society of the Southern states, however, the exploitation is unusually mild, and the slaveowner combines in himself the interests of capital and labor; therefore the class struggle does not develop. In the society of the Northern states, as in all modern industrial societies, the conflict between capital and labor grows more and more intense; it must eventuate in a revolutionary crisis. The only way to prevent revolution, and at the same time to permit extension of the suffrage, is to put into effect the principle of the concurrent majority. This will enable the planters and the capitalists, whose interests are fundamentally the same, to adjust their differences and collaborate against their common foe, the rising proletariat. If, however, Northern property owners persist in refusing to see the only means of their own salvation, the Southern slaveowners will have to take increasingly drastic measures to save themselves.

The *dual presidency*, in addition to nullification, is one possibility for giving the slaveowners an absolute veto. They would have as their tribune a second President, representing the South. Failing such a guarantee, secession may become necessary as a last resort.

Part 3

SIGNIFICANCE AND INFLUENCE

As he worked out his theory of government, Calhoun convinced himself that he had hit upon fundamental truths, and he felt a sense of bafflement whenever he failed to convince others. Tirelessly he would repeat his argument, in or out of the Senate chamber, speaking in his harsh and toneless voice, with stiff, pump-handle gestures, and speaking very fast, faster than any of his colleagues, at a rate of about two hundred words a minute.[1] Very few of his listeners ever doubted the conviction, the sincerity, that propelled this barrage of words, but a number of his hearers did question his line of reasoning, that is, the accuracy of his aim.

When opposing the Force Bill, at the time of South Carolina's nullification attempt, in 1833, he patiently went through his explanation of what sovereignty was and why it was indivisible. "It is the supreme power of the State," he said, "and we might as well speak of half a square, or half a triangle, as half a sovereignty." One of his fellow Senators, John M. Clayton, of Delaware, like him a graduate of both Yale College and the Litchfield law school, objected to this "metaphysical reasoning" and he said he could not comprehend it. Calhoun replied to the senator from Delaware:

If by metaphysics he means the scholastic refinement which makes distinctions without difference, no one can hold it in more utter contempt than I do; but if, on the contrary, he means the power of analysis and combination—that power which reduces the most complex idea into its elements, which traces causes to their first principle and, by the power of generalization and combination, unites the whole in one harmonious system—then, so far from deserving contempt, it is the highest attribute of the human mind. It is the power which raises man above the brute—which distinguishes his faculties from mere sagacity, which he holds in common with inferior animals. It is this power which has raised the astronomer from being a mere gazer at the stars to the high intellectual eminence of a Newton or a Laplace, and astronomy itself from a mere observation of insulated facts into that noble science which displays to our admiration the system of the universe. And shall this high power of the mind, which has effected such wonders when directed to the laws which control the material world, be for ever prohibited, under a senseless cry of metaphysics, from being applied to the high purpose of political science and legislation? I hold them to be subject to laws as fixed as matter itself, and to be as fit a subject for the application of the highest intellectual power. Denunciation may, indeed, fall upon the philosophical inquirer into these first principles, as it did upon Galileo and Bacon when they first unfolded the great discoveries which have been immortalized with their names; but the time will come when truth will prevail in spite of prejudice and denunciation, and when politics and legislation will be considered as much a science as astronomy and chemistry.[2]

Obviously Calhoun already thought of himself as the Newton, the Galileo, of political science.

Two years later the deaf but indefatigably inquiring

Englishwoman Harriet Martineau was in Washington, with her ear trumpet. In her parlor she received many of the capital's celebrities, including the illustrious trio Henry Clay, Daniel Webster, and Calhoun. She recalled:

Mr. Calhoun, the cast-iron man, who looks as if he had never been born and never could be extinguished, would come in sometimes to keep our understandings upon a painful stretch for a short while, and leave us to take to pieces his close, rapid, theoretical illustrated talk, and see what we could make of it. . . . His mind has long lost all power of communicating with any other. I know of no man who lives in such utter intellectual solitude. He meets men, and harangues them by the fireside as in the Senate; he is wrought like a piece of machinery, set going vehemently by a weight, and stops while you answer; he either passes by what you say, or twists it into a suitability with what is in his head, and begins to lecture again. . . . Mr. Calhoun is as full as ever of his nullification doctrines; and those who know the force that is in him, and his utter incapacity of modification by other minds (after having gone through as remarkable a revolution of political opinion as perhaps any man ever experienced) will no more expect repose and self-retention from him than from a volcano in full force. Relaxation is no longer in the power of his will. I never saw any one who so completely gave me the idea of possession.[3]

In some respects Miss Martineau exaggerated. Intellectually Calhoun was not quite so lonesome as she thought. True, he failed to communicate as he wished with the representatives of Northern business. Already, however, he possessed a large following among his contemporaries, especially in the South. A decade after his death he was to influence events as much as he had done while still alive. And after the lapse of almost a century he was at last to be hailed (by others besides his immediate followers) as the great, original political scientist that he had considered himself.

THE USES OF LOGIC

To some extent Calhoun was justified in priding himself, as he did, on his scientific and logical approach to politics. Probably he was the most systematic thinker among the active American politicians of his time. His argument was, and remains, persuasive. Once his assumptions are granted, his reasoning proceeds pretty well from one step to another, and his conclusions follow almost, but not quite, irresistibly. Thus his basic postulates regarding sovereignty lead to his conception of the constitutional compact, and this in turn to his position on nullification, secession, and slavery in the territories.

Even if his assumptions be accepted, however, his argument reveals gaps, inconsistencies, contradictions, and downright errors once it is closely examined. If his assumptions are challenged, the whole structure begins to shake. And if they are rejected, it falls in a heap.

Consider his thinking with regard to sovereignty. This is a protean abstraction, one that can take a variety of shapes. For the sake of the argument, let us accept his own definition (which, of course, is also Bodin's and Blackstone's): Sovereignty is the supreme authority, the ultimate and indivisible source of power within a body politic.

Calhoun dealt with sovereignty, as thus defined, in

historical and legalistic terms. He maintained (as we have seen) that before the Revolution, sovereignty over the thirteen colonies had been lodged in the British Crown. When the colonies became independent, that rare essence automatically passed to the peoples of the states—not in one lump but in thirteen separate pieces. Thus, according to his own reasoning, sovereignty had been divided even though, by his definition, it could not be! Here, at the outset, was an inconsistency which he apparently never recognized and certainly never acknowledged.

He was taking a concept that had been invented to defend the divine right of kings and he was using it to defend the divine right of slaveowners. But he never saw the concept as a mere human invention. To him it was fixed, unchanging, in both meaning and content. He could conceivably have looked upon it differently—as an idea that is relative to time and place and that changes with economic, social, and political change. Viewed as a changing concept—and a changing reality—sovereignty might very well have resided in the separate states at a time when the country was predominantly agricultural, transportation comparatively poor, and the sense of nationality only beginning to develop. Then, with the economic and psychological transformation that the nineteenth century brought, sovereignty itself might have been transformed. That is, the source of power might have entered into a process of diffusion from the people of the states to the people of the nation as a whole—or, rather, from politically conscious and active groups within the states to groups whose membership and interests cut across state lines.

If Calhoun had looked at sovereignty that way, however, the concept would not have served his purpose. The question he asked himself was essentially this: Where *ought* sovereignty to reside if viewed in the abstract (but always with the concrete interests of the slaveholders in the back of the mind)? He might have asked himself a different question: Where in the United States today does sovereignty in fact reside? From his own experience with the nullification effort of 1832–33 he might well have concluded that supreme and ultimate authority actually lay somewhere in back of the federal government—if indeed it could be found to lie all in one piece anywhere.

If it must be discussed, sovereignty need not necessarily be defined as a fixed abstraction. It can also be defined in a more or less concrete, relative, and functional sense. That is, it can be considered as the operating source, or sources, of governmental power in a given situation. To suppose that sovereignty is what Calhoun said it was, and only what he said it was, requires an act of faith.

In his application of the concept he ran into confusion. He confounded the "sovereign community" with the various "interests" of the community, and these he neither listed nor described. Surely he did not mean that each major interest group in the country was sovereign, and yet he contended that each should have a veto on government policy. Nullification and the dual presidency were the only constitutional devices that he proposed for giving effect to this veto. Nullification he based on the supposed sovereignty of the people of each state. In many if not most states, however, the people could divide into a number of groupings, depending on the issue at stake. Obviously, nullification by the sovereign community would not protect all the interests within the state when these were divided. As for the idea of a dual presidency, it did not follow logically from the concept of state sovereignty. Even less effectively than nullification would the dual presidency have safeguarded a particu-

lar interest—except, of course, for the slaveholding interest.

Again, Calhoun ran into difficulty in trying to justify
the new states as sovereign communities. Even conceding that the original thirteen were separately sovereign
—that they somehow had received the magic touch
from the British Crown—there remains the problem of
the states subsequently admitted to the Union. Take
Louisiana as an example. In the case of Louisiana,
as in the case of other territories, Congress passed
an "enabling act" authorizing the people to hold a
convention and draw up a state constitution. Then,
approving the new constitution, Congress declared
the territory to be a state. According to Calhoun's
theory, the people of Louisiana now were sovereign, like the people of South Carolina itself. The
moment before, however, as the people of a mere
territory, they had not been sovereign. Questions arise.
If at first they were not blessed with sovereignty, how
could they have made their own constitution? Then,
when they suddenly acquired the blessing, how did
they get it? Congress could not have conferred it upon
them, for Congress did not have it to confer. The existing states could not have handed it over, by way of
Congress, since it was indivisible and nontransferable.
From these dilemmas Calhoun never managed to escape.[4]

He was caught in yet another dilemma. He aimed,
ostensibly, to protect minorities from the majority, but
he failed to consider that one man's minority may be
another man's majority. Thus, in 1832–33, the South
Carolina nullifiers were a minority in the country as
a whole but a majority in their own state, and opposed
to them was a sizable minority of South Carolina
Unionists. In the Senate, when Calhoun presented his
case for nullification, Webster challenged him: "Look
to South Carolina at the present moment. How far are

the rights of minorities there respected?" Plainly the nullificationist majority was proceeding with a "relentless disregard" for the rights of the Unionist minority—"a minority embracing, as the gentleman himself will admit, a large portion of the wealth and respectability of the state." [5] Calhoun never answered that poser, never explained how minority rights in his own state were protected by nullification.

Each interest group is composed of smaller groups, and each minority is composed of other minorities. If Calhoun's veto principle were carried to its logical conclusion, the minority within any group could nullify the decisions of the majority within that group. This minority could be viewed as yet another group, consisting of its own majority and minority, and within this group again the minority could check the majority. On it would go until the group in question was the smallest that could possibly contain a majority and a minority, and in this group of three the one could negative the other two. The result would be anarchy.

Relentlessly logical though he aspired to be, Calhoun did not press the argument to that point. When he spoke of the "concurrent majority"—the majority of each of the interests—he had in mind only the great interests, only the important ones, but he provided no means of identifying these. More precisely, he was concerned with but a single interest, the slavery interest.

He rationalized as much as he reasoned, and his wish often was the father of his thought. An example of his wishful thinking is his conclusion that the "negative power" would strengthen rather than weaken a government. If this were true, the United Nations, with its big-power veto in the Security Council, ought to be far more cohesive and cooperative than it actually is. Indeed, it ought to be one of the most effective political institutions in the world today. Of course,

Calhoun did not have the example of the U.N. to give him pause, but he did have the example of the one-time Polish government with its *liberum veto*. From that historical example—where the veto power induced no more harmony than in the U.N.—he drew a conclusion quite opposite to the only one that the facts would seem to warrant.

In developing his argument, which in part he based on history, Calhoun at other points also was careless of his historical facts. To prove that the Constitution was a proslavery compact, he asserted that in the summer of 1787, both the Confederation Congress and the Constitutional Convention had been assembled in Philadelphia. This assertion strengthened his argument that there had been an understanding between the Congress and the Convention—the Congress prohibiting slavery in the Northwest Territory and the Convention arranging for the return of fugitive slaves from one state to another. In truth, the Congress at that time was meeting in New York, not in Philadelphia, and there exists no historical evidence for the kind of understanding that Calhoun imagined.

He further contended (as has been seen) that, historically, there had been a fundamental difference between the legislating and the ratifying powers of the states. He held that the lawmaking function belonged to the legislatures and the constitution-making power to the people of the states, who acted through ratifying conventions. As a matter of historical record, however, most of the states, when they made their constitutions during and after the Revolution, did so by the action of their legislatures alone.

At times Calhoun was careless in his reading of the Constitution itself, despite his devotion to that document. He based his nullification procedure upon the amending process, but he slighted one of the two processes by which, according to the Constitution, a state can ratify a constitutional amendment. The two alternatives involve the state legislature and a state convention, the one or the other. That is, the legislature, as well as a convention, can ratify an amendment. Therefore, if nullification is to be based on the amending process, the legislature instead of a convention ought to be able to nullify a federal law. But Calhoun never drew this conclusion, for by doing so he would have weakened the distinction, so fundamental to his whole theory, between the lawmaking and the constitution-making power.

Indeed, he contradicted himself in his basic attitude toward the Constitution. In one sense he was the strictest of strict constructionists, and in another sense the loosest of liberal interpreters. He insisted that the Constitution provides for and permits nothing except what it sets forth in so many words. The document, for instance, nowhere says that Congress can levy duties *for the purpose of encouraging manufactures*, and therefore a protective tariff, according to him, is unconstitutional. So, on the one hand, he could see nothing in the Constitution except what was specifically and clearly stated there. Yet, on the other hand, he could and did find things that were not written into the document and that most Americans could not discover in it. The Father of the Constitution himself, James Madison, who was still alive when Calhoun began to propound the nullification doctrine, could find no constitutional justification for the doctrine.[6] In effect, Calhoun denied "implied powers" to the federal government but claimed implied powers for the states. He pretended that his whole system was derived from the Constitution; it was already there, by implication; all he had done was to draw it out and develop it. What he actually did appears to be what many other Americans have done: he discovered in the fundamental law just what he wanted to find.

The conclusion can only be that logic was Calhoun's slave and not his master. Actually he concerned himself with only one interest and with only one minority. And he ended about where he started, inside a narrow circle bounded by the notion of man's ownership by man.

CONSERVATIVE AND REACTIONARY: WEBSTER AND CALHOUN

Among his contemporaries, Calhoun was not the only politician who thought of himself as a conservative. Webster was another. He, like Calhoun, condemned the notion of rule by mere numbers, wished to safeguard property rights from the envy of majorities, and looked with disapproval (though with less horror than Calhoun) upon the activities of abolitionists. Yet he developed a quite different political philosophy.

Ironically, on the subject of class conflict, as on that of national powers, the Webster of the years *before* 1828 had ideas similar to those of Calhoun *after* 1828. The two men changed positions on social as well as constitutional theory.

In 1820, as an advocate of New England's commercial interests, Webster opposed the protective tariff on the grounds that it was both unconstitutional and unwise. It was unwise, he said, repeating familiar *laissez-faire* arguments, because it would lead to "too much reliance on government" and to a "perpetual contest" between the "different interests of society" as farmers and manufacturers and shipowners all lobbied for special favors in Washington. Far better, he believed, to "leave men to their own discretion" and let them "employ their capital and labor in such occupations as they themselves found most expedient."

He went on to say he was not "advancing any agrarian notions," any revolutionary ideas, but he thought "those employments which tended to make the poor both more numerous and more poor, and the rich less in number, but perhaps more rich, were not employments for us to encourage by taxing other employments." And this he believed would be "the tendency of the manufacturing system pushed to excess," for "manufacturing capital came in the end to be owned but by few." Having no property and no respectability, factory workers would have no "stake in society." Once they had grown numerous enough they would oppose "laws made for the protection of property," would look on other men's possessions as "prey and plunder," and would be "ready, at all times, for violence and revolution." [7]

With the adoption of the protective system, and with the continued growth of manufactures, signs of dangerous class feeling did indeed appear during the 1830's. In Boston a Workingmen's party, most of whose members were said to be actually of the "middling class," campaigned with slogans of hostility to the business group that dominated New England. In New York the "Workies" went to even greater extremes; the more radical among them demanded an "agrarian law" for sharing the wealth through a periodic division of private property. Commenting on these men of the *extrême gauche,* the English traveler Thomas Hamilton wrote in 1833 that, as yet, they were neither numerous nor widespread, but he predicted that their party would multiply throughout the nation as population increased and wages fell.[8]

To many Americans of the 1830's, political campaigns began to look like battles in a class war. The class-conscious workingmen formed a faction, the Loco Focos, within the Democratic party. The party's leaders, even Andrew Jackson himself, seemed to endorse the view that politics had become a struggle between the poor and the rich. In vetoing the recharter of the Bank of the United States, for example, Jackson condemned the bank as a monopoly which made the rich richer and the poor poorer, and which threatened to overpower the people's government itself. The onset of depression, after the Panic of 1837, intensified the class feelings of those who suffered most, the unemployed.

During the 1840's the Jacksonians continued to present their party and their policies as the means of salvation for the laboring man. Robert J. Walker, Secretary of the Treasury in the cabinet of James K. Polk, urged that tariff rates be reduced in order that hapless workers might be saved from greedy capitalists and the nation as a whole might be spared the horrors of class struggle. Walker argued:

> As the profit of capital invested in manufactures is augmented by the protective tariff, there is a corresponding increase of power, until the control of such capital over the wages of labor becomes irresistible. As this power is exercised from time to time we find it resisted by combinations among the working classes by turning out for higher wages or for shorter time; by trades-unions; and in some countries unfortunately by violence and bloodshed. But the government by protective duties arrays itself on the side of the manufacturing system, and by thus augmenting its wealth and power soon terminates in its favor the struggle between man and man—between capital and labor.[9]

The Jacksonian radicals often talked of revolutionary dangers but seldom advocated revolutionary violence. Instead they proposed the elimination of government

favors to private enterprise, the destruction of govern-
ment-granted monopolies and other corporate priv-
ileges, which supposedly were to blame for economic
inequality and popular distress. The radical impetus
came largely from artisans, shopkeepers, and small
businessmen, who assumed that, if freed from governmental interference, they would prosper in just proportion to their own individual efforts. These devotees of
laissez faire took essentially the same position that
Webster had taken in 1820.

But Webster had changed his mind since then. During the 1830's and 1840's he upheld the "American
System" that Henry Clay earlier had proposed and
Calhoun once had supported. This was a program
of government intervention in the economy by means
of protective tariffs, a national bank, and expenditures
for internal improvements. Webster worked out a ra-
tionale for justifying such intervention on social as
well as constitutional grounds. According to his new
philosophy, class conflict was not inevitable; class harmony could be realized through the proper exercise
of government powers.

Replying to the Democrats, Webster said they did
an "extreme injustice" when they attacked the tariff
as favoring "the rich corporations of New England."
He insisted, much as Alexander Hamilton earlier had
done, that it favored the workingman just as much, for
it would "induce capitalists to invest their capital in
such a manner as to occupy and employ American labor." Indeed, the tariff also would benefit the planters
of the South and farmers everywhere, for it would
create a home market in which they could profitably
sell their produce. The tariff "favors every interest in
the country"—manufacturing "is not an exclusive but
a general interest." By fostering this general interest,
the federal government could advance and reconcile
the interests of all. It could make everyone prosperous

and give even the workingman a sizable stake in society. All or practically all the citizens being property
owners, all could safely be entrusted with the ballot,
if they received the kind of moral, religious, and constitutional teachings which would make them immune
to the arguments of self-interested agitators.

From 1776 on, according to Webster, American history had been "marked by a peculiar conservatism."
The government was based upon the will of the people, but in their state constitutions and in the federal
Constitution the people had agreed to *"limit themselves."* They had secured their government against
"the sudden impulses of mere majorities." The people
could continue to enjoy self-government and equal
rights so long as they remembered that "freedom from
restraint is not FREEDOM" and that a "general scramble
which leads the idle and the extravagant to hope for a
time when they may put their hands into their neigh-
bors' pockets, call it what you please, is tyranny."

Thus Webster shared some of the same fear that Calhoun had for the tyranny of the majority, yet Webster
saw no need for the drastic remedies that Calhoun
proposed. Webster was confident that the representative system itself would provide security enough for
men of property so long as the system was correctly
understood and applied, and so long as property remained widely distributed.[10]

Nor did Webster take the pessimistic view that Calhoun did when he looked to the consequences of con-
tinuing industrial development. Webster thought the
new technology would be a great leveler, a great har-
monizer, a bringer of social happiness as well as
material comfort, rather than a cause of widening class
differences and worsening class conflict. He could not
find praise enough for "this mighty agent, steam." He
said, in 1847:

It lessens labor, it economizes time, it gives the poor man leisure and ability to travel, it joins the most remote regions and brings their inhabitants face to face, establishing a harmony of interest and feeling between them. It limits all distinctions. The poor and the rich, the prince and the peasant, enjoy now equal facilities of travel, and can procure the same comforts and luxuries from distant points, and when they travel they sit side by side in the same rail-car. The individual is sinking, and the mass rising up in the majesty of common manhood.[11]

In the utopian conservatism of Webster, mechanical invention could overcome class, sectional, and international conflicts if men would but encourage it and give it time.

The Webster view was essentially the same as that of most Whigs during the years—about twenty—that they stayed together as a national party. Theirs was a party of the plantation as well as the corporation, and it included most of the richest men in the country, South as well as North. It never included Calhoun, though from 1833 to 1837 he cooperated with the Whig leaders in resisting the "usurpations" of Andrew Jackson. The Whig organization was, in one of its aspects, an alliance of planters and capitalists, but it was not quite the kind of alliance that Calhoun desired.

From his standpoint there were two things wrong with the Whigs. First, they advocated policies, such as the tariff, which he considered harmful to planter interests. Second, they justified these policies by exalting the discretionary powers of the federal government, thus encouraging the abolitionists to believe that they could use its powers to bring about, sooner or later, the destruction of slavery.

From Calhoun's point of view the Democratic party

also had its faults. While Jackson was President, the Democrats seemed as bad as the Whigs in aggrandizing the powers of the federal government. The Democrats were even worse than the Whigs in emphasizing the rights of the common man and thus spreading the false doctrine of natural equality.

So Calhoun could not feel quite at home, spiritually, with either the Whigs or the Democrats. He had repudiated the basic faith of most members of both parties, the faith that men are born with equal opportunities and equal rights. In his philosophical assumptions he stood to the right of the Whig conservatives and far to the right of the Democratic radicals. Really he was neither the one nor the other: he was a reactionary. He reacted against, instead of seeking an accommodation with, the trend of American thought from 1776 on. He harked back to the principles of an earlier and less egalitarian time.

When he joined the Democrats, during the Van Buren Administration, he did so for reasons of expediency, not principle. His fundamental beliefs he did not abandon. He effected a *rapprochement* of reactionaries with radicals inside the Democratic party. Against this meeting of extremes, Webster and the Whigs defended a conservative middle ground.

As the extremes of right and left came together against the center, Democrats denounced the corporation but praised the plantation, condemned the employers of wage labor but supported the owners of slaves. The Democrats did this both in Washington and in the state capitals of the North. At the Pennsylvania constitutional convention of 1837–38, for example, the Loco Foco delegates contended that all corporations were "unrepublican and radically wrong," that "labor performed for corporations was like the labor of slaves," and that, if Northern abolitionists were allowed to go South and stir up slaves against masters, then Southern agitators would be justified in coming North and arousing employees against employers.

As a Whig delegate to the Pennsylvania convention, Thaddeus Stevens expressed his horror at this suggestion and referred sarcastically to the "appropriate alliance" being formed "between the radical reformers of the North and the lawless nullifiers of the South." Then and afterward Stevens tried to break up this alliance and win the common man to the support of business interests by identifying antislavery with democracy and the slavery regime with aristocracy.[12]

In the United States Senate, Webster played down the question of slavery. He made his central theme the potential harmony of all interests and all classes. What was good for the businessmen of Boston and New York and Philadelphia, he repeated again and again, was good for everybody, rich and poor, North and South. "In the old countries of Europe there is a clear and well-defined line between capital and labor," he conceded to Calhoun and the radicals. But he denied that there was a line so "broad, marked, and visible" in the United States. Who in this country were laborers, and who capitalists? Why, he said, practically all Americans (he meant Northerners) belonged to the "working classes" or the "industrious classes," and he included in these groups the "active men of business." Only those very few who lived exclusively on income from property were "capitalists." The Democrats who "would teach the laborer that he is but an oppressed slave" were insulting the Northern people as a whole.

The antislavery cause, which Webster eschewed but some other Whigs took up, was eventually to split the party between North and South and divide the Northern remnant into two factions, one devoted to "conscience" and the other to "cotton." Webster became a "cotton" Whig. After the death of Calhoun and the passage of the Compromise of 1850, the "conscience" Whigs began to combine with the Free-Soil Democrats. Webster now (1851–52) proposed a "remodelling of parties" so as to combine Northern and Southern conservatives, on the one side, in opposition to antislavery liberals on the other. "There must be a Union Party," he said, "& an opposing party under some name, I know not what, very likely the Party of Liberty." As Secretary of State in Millard Fillmore's cabinet, Webster did his best, or his worst, to give effect to the constitutional guarantees of slavery by enforcing drastically the new federal fugitive-slave act.[13]

Thus, at the very end of his career, Webster seemed about to come around to Calhoun's long-cherished view that men of property, North and South, should make common cause against radicalism in all its forms. It was too late to make an effective combination of this kind. The forces of sectionalism had become too strong. And Calhoun, more than any other one person, had brought about the sectionalization of the country, the unification of the South. Sectional war was to follow. This was not what Calhoun had wished, but it was what, in the absence of a comprehensive reactionary-conservative alliance, he had felt he must prepare for.

FROM JEFFERSON TO JEFFERSON DAVIS

When, at last, the sections separated and the war came, leaders on both sides appealed to the spirit of Thomas Jefferson. President Davis, in launching the Confederacy, and President Lincoln, in calling for its destruction, quoted the Declaration of Independence. They seemed to agree that certain truths were self-evident, but not the same truths. Lincoln picked out the proposition that "all men are created equal" and

Davis the proposition that they have an "inalienable" right to abandon one government and adopt another.[14] The Confederate Vice-President, Alexander H. Stephens, repeated the name of Jefferson, like a refrain, in a speech frankly declaring that the Confederacy had for its "corner stone" the principle of human inequality.

Thus, in 1861, the long-dead Jefferson appeared to contradict himself. He was made to speak for a libertarian, egalitarian philosophy and at the same time for a secessionist doctrine which was inconsistent with such a philosophy. As a young man, however, in the years before 1800, he had used state-rights arguments in pursuit of liberal, not illiberal ends. In the Kentucky Resolutions (1798–99), for example, he proposed that the state legislatures act as "sentinels" and, if necessary, resort to nullification so as to protect their citizens from repressive measures of the federal government— in this case the Alien and Sedition Acts. There was, in those days, no contradiction between Jeffersonian localism and Jeffersonian liberalism.

By 1861 something had happened, in the South, to the old ideas of Jeffersonian democracy. The state-rights doctrine had been detached from the liberal principle and joined to a reactionary one. The ideals of freedom-loving farmers were adapted to the interests of slaveholding planters, and the party of Jefferson was transformed into the party of Jefferson Davis. Between these two men stood two others who handed on the torch and altered its fuel and its flame as they did so. One was John Randolph of Roanoke. The other and much the more significant was Calhoun. In helping thus to make Jefferson the light of illiberalism, Calhoun left his most important mark upon the development of American political thought.[15]

Jefferson himself had assisted the process. In 1820 the controversy over the admission of Missouri as a slave state awakened him, as he said, "like a fire-bell in the night." While Calhoun, then still in his nationalist phase, approved the Missouri Compromise as a means of holding the Union together, Jefferson feared that the feelings of antislavery, or "anti-Missourianism," newly aroused, would lead to a division of the country along a moral line and, ultimately, to civil war. He wished to prevent the spread of such dangerous feelings. Already the University of Virginia, the favorite project of his old age, was under construction. He hoped that this university would attract, from the entire South, students who otherwise might attend Northern colleges and become indoctrinated with "lessons of anti-Missourianism." [16] At one time he had looked upon education as a means of liberating the human mind; now he began to look upon it also as a means of protecting slavery.

His blood relative and erstwhile disciple, John Randolph, already had tied slavery to state rights. In the early 1800's Randolph parted from Jefferson and accused him of betraying his own principles of strict construction. He thought of himself as more Jeffersonian than Jefferson, and certainly he was more consistent in opposing the exercise of powers the Constitution had not specifically granted to the federal government. During and after the War of 1812, which he condemned, Randolph had no use for such nationalists as Calhoun and Clay. Meanwhile he undertook to organize the South and, in the words of Henry Adams, to "array the whole slaveholding influence behind the banner of states' rights." He did not believe in nullification, but he was glad to see anything done that might solidify the South and protect the planters. When South Carolina nullified, he applauded. He died soon after.[17]

Belatedly, in 1837, Calhoun paid his respects to Randolph. He now believed that the Missouri Compromise (which excluded slavery from part of the territories) had been a "dangerous measure," he said. If all Southerners had opposed it as determinedly as Randolph had done, "abolition might have been crushed for ever in its birth." But, Calhoun confessed, he himself at that time had considered Randolph "too unyielding, too uncompromising, too impracticable." Since then, he had been "taught his error." [18] Certainly he owed much to Randolph—though Henry Adams goes too far in saying: "All that was ablest and most masterly, all except what was mere metaphysical rubbish, in Calhoun's statesmanship had been suggested by Randolph years before Calhoun began his states'-rights career." [19]

In demanding that all the territories be left open to slavery, Calhoun claimed to be on the side of Jefferson as well as Randolph. He quoted Jefferson's "fire-bell in the night" letter when opposing the application of the Wilmot Proviso to the Oregon Territory, in 1848.[20] Throughout his career, he refrained from open disagreement with Jefferson, and though he often denounced the "all men are created equal" phrase, he never condemned its author. Again and again he harked back to the "principles of '98," meaning the Jeffersonian principles of the Kentucky Resolutions, which he considered as authority for his own doctrine of state rights.

Calhoun acted in the spirit of Randolph and of the later Jefferson when he tried to unite Southerners by telling them that, unless they got together, slavery would be doomed. Finally, during the winter of 1849–50, he led the way toward the union of the South and the disunion of the nation by bringing about the call for a convention of the Southern states. This convention was to consider cooperative action, and possibly secession, in case the delegates should conclude that the Compromise of 1850, when it reached its final form, provided inadequate guarantees for the interests of the South.

While Calhoun lay on his deathbed, in March, 1850, his enemy Francis P. Blair wrote: "This is his euthanasia, for 'tis given out that having completed the ground work he does not look to live to enjoy it—poor old man, he resolved to die in giving birth to the Southern Confederacy." [21] Five days later he was dead. Not till more than ten years later was the Southern Confederacy to be born. Calhoun was not its immediate parent but rather its grandparent in the line of descent from Jefferson and Randolph.

The next in the line was to be Jefferson Davis. He was one of a group of senators who accompanied Calhoun's body from Washington to its burial place in Charleston. "Then he had been the most admired Southerner among the living," one of Davis' biographers has written, "and South Carolina had helped to drape the mantle of her illustrious son around his shoulders." [22] But Davis did not keep the mantle on, or at least he did not, for the time being, display its secessionist lining. During the 1850's he reenacted a phase of Calhoun's earlier career. Like Calhoun, he was a great Secretary of War (1853–57) and used the office to promote transportation improvements. Like Calhoun, he hoped to become President of the United States, and he devoted himself not to secession but to sectional unity within the national union. He was later to emerge as a leader of the movement for the secession and confederation of the South.

Meanwhile the Southern forces remained disorganized and, in an overall sense, leaderless. No one took over Calhoun's following and carried it, intact, through the decade after his death. In 1850 the extreme Secessionists of South Carolina, such as Robert Barnwell Rhett, did not look upon themselves as successors of Calhoun. Preferring immediate action by the separate states, Rhett opposed the Calhoun project for a Southern convention to make cooperative plans.[23] And certainly the South Carolina Unionists, such as Benjamin F. Perry, did not follow in the Calhoun tradition. "I regard his death as fortunate for the country & his own fame," Perry noted in his diary. "The slavery question will now be settled. He would have been an obstacle in the way." [24]

A Northern jurist expressed a quite different view. "Mr. Calhoun's death has deified his opinions," this Northerner wrote in June, 1850, "and he is therefore more dangerous dead than living." [25] The opinions of Calhoun were made generally available through the publication of his works between 1852 and 1855. These opinions continued to influence, though they did not determine, the thinking of the Southern politicians who eventualy brought about disunion.

In the ongoing debate over slavery in the territories, Southerners followed the Calhoun line of argument only in part. They still maintained, as he had done, that the fugitive-slave clause was part of a bargain that had induced the South to ratify the Constitution. They still maintained, also, that Congress as a "trustee" must, in legislating for the territories, give effect to state laws with respect to slavery. But the Southerners now exalted the authority of the Supreme Court in a way that Calhoun had never done (though he probably would have done the same had he lived to see the Court become the slavery bulwark that it became in the 1850's). Moreover, in giving opinions favorable to slavery, Chief Justice Roger B. Taney made no use of Calhoun's notion that sovereignty was indivisible and belonged solely to the peoples of the separate states. Quite the contrary. Taney reasoned from an assumption of divided sovereignty in both the Dred Scott case (1857), upholding the Calhoun doctrine of a congressional trusteeship for the territories, and the case of *Ableman* v. *Booth* (1859), asserting the Calhoun position that a state, in this instance Wisconsin, could not constitutionally obstruct the enforcement of the federal fugitive-slave law.[26] While Southerners denounced the kind of nullification that Wisconsin had attempted, none of them during the 1850's proposed the Calhoun version of nullification as a remedy for the South.

With the coming of the crisis of 1860–61, however, Calhoun reemerged as a leading prophet (second only to Jefferson and Davis) of the disaffected Southerners. From his place in the Senate, Davis strove in 1860 to force an extreme proslavery candidate and platform upon the Democratic party. He worked with President James Buchanan and with the fire-eater William L. Yancey to prevent Southerners from supporting Stephen A. Douglas, the champion of "popular sovereignty" for the territories. Davis now reread Calhoun's proslavery and state-rights resolutions of 1837 and attempted to make these the party's resolutions of 1860. "The South demanded the recognition of the 'new Calhounism' as the doctrine which the country must accept," as William E. Dodd has written, "the alternative, in the minds of men like Yancey of Alabama and Rhett of South Carolina and A. G. Brown of Mississippi, being secession." [27]

South Carolina, the home state of Calhoun, was, quite fittingly, the first to leave the Union. The Secessionists in this state, as in the states that followed her example, based their action on his theory that the people, as a sovereign community, had acceded to the constitutional compact and by the same procedure, in reverse, could secede from it. They did not do violence to his opinions when, complaining of the personal-liberty laws, they justified their decision on the grounds that thirteen Northern states had "enacted laws which either nullify the Acts of Congress or render useless any attempt to execute them," for Calhoun too had denounced that kind of nullification. When Davis advised his own state of Mississippi to secede, shortly after South Carolina had done so, he echoed Calhoun in saying he never would have recommended separation if "the principles of the Union, under the Constitution, had been faithfully adhered to by all the Parties to it." [28]

Newspapers North and South looked upon secession as an application and a test of Calhoun's political philosophy. The *Columbia Guardian,* for example, printed a letter from a group of South Carolina cadets at West Point who rejoiced that their state was proceeding to organize for herself "a new and separate government (a government of which our beloved Calhoun would approve were he with us at this time)." [29] The *Philadelphia Press* raised the question whether South Carolina could, on any constitutional ground, prevent the enforcement of federal laws within her limits. "If that be admitted, then the old exploded heresy of nullification of Mr. Calhoun is right, and it follows that General Jackson and Henry Clay and Daniel Webster and Edward Livingston and all that class of great statesmen were wrong." [30]

Though the Southerners applied Calhoun's principles in seceding, they did not follow them consistently in forming their new, Confederate government. The Confederate constitution acknowledged in so many words the sovereignty of the states but not the right of nullification or secession. The constitution did guarantee slavery. It forbade the Congress to abolish it, and it required each state to recognize and protect the slave property of visitors, temporary or permanent, from other states; so, in effect, it prevented the states as well as the Congress from bringing slavery to an end. Essentially, then, the constitution conformed to the spirit, if not the letter, of the teachings of Calhoun. With him, the protection of slavery had always been the constant; the constitutional means had been the variable.

To wage war effectively, the Confederate government needed to act with vigor. Some of the states, especially Georgia and North Carolina, objected to the conscription laws and other war measures of the Confederacy. Alexander H. Stephens, once a Whig and a friend of Lincoln's, became a fanatical advocate of state rights. Jefferson Davis, always a Democrat, a fellow partisan of Calhoun's, the inheritor of his "mantle," came to be denounced as a consolidationist and a despot. Now Stephens took over the role of Calhoun —and Davis, at least in Stephens' view, the role of Andrew Jackson!

After the war both Stephens and Davis turned to constructing elaborate rationalizations of their respective careers. Each wrote a long, two-volume *apologia,* and each used Calhoun's works as a text.

Stephens minimized his wartime differences with Davis and maximized his faithfulness to Calhoun. He quoted him extensively. At one point he remarked:

Amongst the many great men with whom he [Stephens] was associated, Mr. Calhoun was by far the most philosophical statesman of them all. Indeed, with the exception of Mr. Jefferson, it may be questioned if in this respect the United States has ever produced his superior. Government he considered a science, and in this subject his whole soul was absorbed. His treatise on the Constitution of the United States is the best that was ever penned upon that subject, and his *Disquisition* on *Government,* generally, is one of the few books of this age that will outlive the language in which it was written.[31]

Stephens entitled his work *A Constitutional View of the Late War between the States* (1868–70). Thus he gave to Southerners the designation by which many of them thereafter would insist that the Civil War be known. This designation, "War Between the States," continues to serve as a reminder that a particular "constitutional view" lay behind the attempt of Southerners to gain their independence.

Davis, in *The Rise and Fall of the Confederate Government* (1881), showed himself to be a somewhat less thorough and less apt student than Stephens. Yet, on the whole, Davis too followed and repeated the Calhoun philosophy, and he too expressed his admiration for the master, for "that pure spirit, luminous intellect, and devoted adherent of the Constitution." [32]

Both Stephens and Davis, in their memoirs, treated as incidental and relatively unimportant the issue that their mentor himself had never blinked—the issue of human slavery. Retrospectively, they had purified the Calhoun theory and, in doing so, had strained out its very essence.

THE NEO-CALHOUNISM
OF THE TWENTIETH CENTURY

After the Civil War the reputation of Calhoun declined. True, Davis praised him, and Stephens declared that his works would live forever, but these men were really looking backward, not forward. In his own state, Calhoun became something of a folk hero. Carolina cotton farmers were heard to say, years after Appomattox, that the South would have won the war if he had been still living when it was fought.[33] He experienced a kind of resurrection when, in 1884, his iron coffin was moved from the temporary grave to a relatively imposing sarcophagus, for which the state finally had appropriated funds.[34] Yet, South as well as North, Calhoun had personified the slave states at war, and those states had been defeated. His theories, it seemed, had been put to the test of battle, and they had failed the test. For Northerners, his name continued to glow with a "lurid intensity," [35] but it was a light from the dead past, a name with evil yet quaint and antiquarian connotations. For Southerners, it was a symbol of defeat.

By the beginning of the twentieth century, Calhoun had lost practically all relevance for living Americans. In 1911 the historian William E. Dodd, himself a Southerner, could write: "No political party looks back to Calhoun as its founder or rejuvenator, no group of public men proclaim allegiance to his doctrines, no considerable group of individuals outside of South Carolina profess any love for his name and ideals." [36]

Suddenly, nearly a hundred years after his death, his reputation recovered and took on new aspects. By the middle of the twentieth century a Calhoun revival was under way. He and his theory seemed timely again.

New biographies came out: a three-volume, nearly definitive life; a "humanized" portrait that won a Pulitzer Prize; and a brief and critical "reappraisal." [37] A book-length study of his political philosophy appeared.[38] His *Disquisition on Government* was reissued again and again, in various editions. A project for publishing his complete writings, in twelve to fifteen volumes, was announced.[39] He was made the subject of dozens of essays, and these were given space not only in learned journals but also in popular periodicals, among them *Harper's Magazine, Time,* and *The Saturday Evening Post.*

More remarkable than the quantity of this writing was the theme of much of it. The authors treated Calhoun as no antiquarian curiosity but a political philosopher with an enduring message and a unique relevance for their time.

The *Harper's* article (1948) asserted, strange though it might seem, that his theory "came through the Civil War stronger than ever." True, Calhoun had been concerned with a veto to protect the interests of slave-holders, but "by implication he would have given a similar veto to every other special interest, whether it be labor, management, the Catholic church, old-age pensioners, the silver miners, or the corn-growers of the Middle West." In a "somewhat elusive sense," the American people actually had adopted this concept of group veto and had put it into practice. "But elusive and subtle as it may be, it remains the basic rule of the game of politics in this country—and in this country alone." In short, Calhoun was the author of the "unwritten rules of American politics" as currently carried on.[40]

Time magazine took up the same theme in reporting the news (1952) that Senator Richard Russell, of Georgia, had announced himself as a contender for the presidential nomination on the Democratic ticket. According to *Time*, Russell thus implied a "latent threat of revolt" which Southern Democrats were using to bargain with their Northern partisans. Here, in operation, was the "concurrent majority" principle of Calhoun. "He meant that every essential group in the nation had a veto on policies directly affecting it." Of course, his veto in the form of nullification was buried with him. "But Calhounism survives in a far more subtle and resilient form than legal nullification," said *Time*. "It was built into the structure of the American party system." It could be found in the give and take of the national nominating convention—"in a great and much maligned American institution, the smoke-filled room." [41]

Herbert Ravenel Sass, identified as a "hopping-mad

Charlestonian," pursued a similar argument in a *Saturday Evening Post* article (1954), in which he complained that Northern writers did less than justice to the history and culture of the South. Sass mentioned Calhoun as a neglected figure of nineteenth-century intellectual history, and the *Disquisition* and *Discourse* as neglected classics. Calhoun's "brilliantly original" exposition of the concurrent majority was "the most revolutionary contribution to political science made by an American," according to Sass, and it was "also the blueprint by which our republic largely operates today." Calhoun had recognized that a free society could not exist as a mass of undifferentiated individuals. It was made up of groups with conflicting interests, and these groups had to have some means of protection against one another. Bringing the theory up to date, Sass explained:

The groups to which Calhoun wished to give formal voice—the labor group, the management group, the farm group, the Southern group and various others—have learned to protect themselves against one another and against the numerical majority and to maintain themselves as separate political elements whose concurrence with the numerical majority must be had in the shaping of legislation. Today the Washington lobbies of the principal interests which make up the republic have become a fully accepted part of the American political mechanism because both the soundness and the indispensability of the principle are tacitly recognized.[42]

Writing in *The New York Times*, Senator Paul H. Douglas, of Illinois, reflected the new interpretation of Calhoun. It is "almost impossible to force through measures that are deeply resented and opposed by any large minority of the population," Douglas noted, in discussing the presidency. "This means that Calhoun's theory of requiring majorities of each significant group in the country to concur before a measure can be passed, while rejected in theory, has nevertheless been largely realized on important matters in practice." [43]

These writers themselves had not rediscovered Calhoun; they were merely paraphrasing others, among them a political scientist, Peter F. Drucker, who had elaborated upon "Calhoun's pluralism" as a "key to American politics" in a professional journal (1948). Drucker contended that "for the constitutional veto power of the states over national legislation, by means of which Calhoun proposed to formalize the principle of sectional and interest compromise, was substituted in actual practice the much more powerful and much more elastic but extra-constitutional veto power of sections, interests, and pressure groups."

According to Drucker, this new veto power, the modern version of the concurrent majority, operated within Congress, the Administration, the national nominating convention, and, above all, the political party. In Congress there were blocs, such as the farm bloc, which could negative measures adversely affecting the groups they represented; and there were lobbies which could check legislation opposed by any of the major interests. In the Administration, some of the cabinet members, such as the secretaries of labor, agriculture, and commerce, looked out for the welfare of special groups. In the selection of a presidential candidate (and also of other candidates) availability or eligibility had to be taken into account: "Eligibility simply means that a candidate must not be unacceptable to any major interest, religious or regional group within the electorate; it is primarily a negative qualification." In the party—which "(rather than the states) has become the instrument to realize Calhoun's 'rule of the concurrent majority' "—the working of the veto was most in evidence: "It [the party] must, by definition, be acceptable equally to the right and the left, the rich and the poor, the farmer and the worker, the Protestant and the Catholic, the native and the foreign-born." [44]

Though he made the most elaborate presentation of the new Calhounism, Drucker did not originate it. Before him, Charles M. Wiltse had put forth the thesis in a couple of published essays (1937 and 1941). Even earlier, V. L. Parrington had suggested the idea. Among the new interpreters, only Wiltse could claim a close acquaintance with Calhoun's career and works. He became the author of the most scholarly and most exhaustive of all Calhoun biographies.

Wiltse maintained that when, in Calhoun's scheme, a state insisted upon its sovereignty, the state was really acting as an economic rather than a geographical unit. Nullification was an assertion of the sovereignty of the interest group, not the state. "To Calhoun they were the same." In his day the negative took the form of state interposition to restrain the enforcement of a federal law. "In terms of the unlocalized economic interests of today, its expressions are strikes, lockouts, injunctions, and the political activities of pressure groups." Congress in the middle of the twentieth century could make no law objectionable to agriculture or industry without these interests finding some way, generally, to modify or nullify the law. So the country had come to have, in fact, a kind of "functional representation." This operated on a principle essentially the same as the concurrent majority of Calhoun. "Today it means that economic legislation should have the approval of labor as well as capital, of consumer as well as producer, of farmer as well as manufacturer." [45]

One of the most extreme statements of Calhoun's relevance for the present was that of another of his biographers, Margaret L. Coit (1950). She averred that Calhoun was the author of "perhaps the most powerful defense of minority rights in a democracy ever written." [46] She had taken her cue from Arthur M. Schlesinger, Jr. "In the end his theory was not a lawyer's brief, adroitly constructed to advance the pretensions of slavery," Schlesinger had written (1945), "but a brilliant and penetrating study of modern society, whose insights remain vital for any minority." [47]

Schlesinger viewed himself as a liberal; among his contemporaries he stood at the opposite extreme from Russell Kirk, a self-styled conservative. The liberal and the conservative could join, however, in admiration of Calhoun. Kirk praised him for his "devotion to freedom" and rated him, along with John Adams, as "one of the two most eminent American political writers." [48]

Wiltse had been cautious enough to say: "Whether or not Calhoun would have conceded that the great unlocalized interests of today fulfill his definition can only be guessed." [49] Indeed, this is more than doubtful, and equally dubious is the description of present-day politics and policymaking that Wiltse and the other neo-Calhounites give. In appraising the new interpretation, then, two questions might be asked. First, does it, with reference to the "veto," accurately describe the political practices of the present? Second, does it really reflect the teachings of Calhoun a century and more ago?

The illustrations the neo-Calhounites use, to demonstrate the "veto" by each interest or each minority today, are plausible but unconvincing. Here is one: "For sixteen years [1932-48] the Republicans lost much of their standing as a truly national party because they had made themselves unacceptable to labor." [50] Thus labor's "veto" did seem to have some effect during those years, but it failed to operate against the Taft-Hartley Act (1947), which the Republican Congress passed despite the last-ditch opposition of labor leaders, who denounced it as a "slave-labor law." And what had happened to labor's "veto" during the preceding twelve years of Republican supremacy? Another example: "Similarly, the Democrats during the middle stage of the New Deal incurred the wrath of the business interests." [51] What became of the *business* "veto" during those sixteen (ultimately twenty) years that the New Dealers were in power? The explanation is offered that President Franklin D. Roosevelt had set aside the "veto" by his appeal to the needs of the "temporary emergency" which the depression had brought. But what does a "veto" amount to if it can be charmed away by a couple of magic words, such as "temporary emergency"? Surely this is not the kind of negative power that Calhoun had in mind!

A third illustration, which the neo-Calhounites use to support their argument, does further damage to their own case. "By 1946 . . . labor troubles could be resolved only on a basis acceptable to both labor and employer: higher wages *and* higher prices." [52] Now, this may illustrate a "veto" by labor and by employer, but it also shows the lack, in this instance, of a "veto" by consumer or by farmer. What the wage-price agreement here amounts to, in fact, is a deal between two interests at the expense of the rest of the community. It is not an agreement arrived at through consultation of all interests.

No doubt this sort of bargaining *is* fairly typical of what actually goes on in the United States. Together with the other examples mentioned, it demonstrates the fact that politicians and pressure groups normally do not appease every minority (not even every big one), do not allow each interest a "veto," do not arrive at action on the basis of unanimity. Instead, they construct a working majority through the combination of several (but not necessarily all) minorities. When, to form the combination, the support of a particular group is needed, the demands of that group, the positive or negative demands, are respected. To the extent, then, that any interest or minority can get concessions from other interests or minorities in the process of forming the majority, to that extent the "veto" of the interest or minority is effective. But only to that extent. The process is familiar enough, and so is the word for it—"logrolling."

This practice is far from new in the history of American politics. In Calhoun's own time there were blocs, lobbies, and factions, and there was logrolling among them. Calhoun himself was aware, painfully aware, of the concessions that both Whig and Democratic politicians were prone to make to tariff lobbyists or to the antislavery or free-soil bloc. He knew from bitter experience what "availability" meant in the choosing of a presidential candidate. He was acquainted with the struggle, essentially the same then as now, by which contending groups sought to get control of the government. "If no one interest be strong enough, of itself, to obtain it," he wrote, "a combination will be formed between those whose interests are most alike—each conceding something to the others, until a sufficient number is obtained to make a majority." [53] That was the essence of the process in his day, and it remains the essence of the process in ours.

But this was not and is not what Calhoun advocated. Quite the contrary. He condemned that kind, the familiar kind, of politics. He thought that by its inevitable tendency "principle and policy would lose all influence in the elections; then cunning, falsehood, deception, slander, fraud, and gross appeals to the appetites of the lowest and most worthless portions of the community would take the place of sound reason and wise debate." [54] Certainly he had no use for the kind of trading that went on at party conventions. He opposed allowing minorities, such as the abolitionists, to exercise any kind of veto on presidential nominations. For example, as he looked forward, in 1847, to the election of the following year, he thought there was a scheme by which slaveholders and abolitionists would be "coerced into nominating and supporting the same candidate" on the Democratic ticket.

> Should it succeed—should the party machinery for President-making prove strong enough to force the slaveholding States to join in a convention to nominate and support a candidate who will be acceptable to the abolitionists, they will have committed the most suicidal act that a people ever perpetrated. I say acceptable; for it is clear that the non-slaveholding States will outnumber in convention the slaveholding, and that no one who is not acceptable to the abolitionists can receive their votes; and, of course, the votes of the States where they hold the balance; and that no other will be nominated, or, if nominated, be elected.

Calhoun went on to denounce all nominating conventions as "irresponsible bodies" which were unknown to the Constitution. He urged Southerners to renounce the forthcoming Democratic convention of 1848 and to unite in a strictly Southern party. The election of the President, he added, ought to be left strictly to the electoral college, as the framers of the Constitution had intended.[55] He refused to be satisfied with the combination of interests upon policy unless *all* interests (that is, all property-owning interests and, in particular, the slavery interest) were consulted and their approval gained. "I am," he declared, "in favor of the government of the whole; the only really and truly popular government—a government based on the concurrent majority—the joint assent of all the parts, through their respective majority of the whole." [56] He insisted upon essential *unanimity* as the condition for governmental action.

This requirement, for all the assertions of the neo-Calhounites, does not exist today. It did not exist when Calhoun was alive. He looked for some means of imposing it; he found the means, constitutionally, in his theory of state rights and, politically, in his plan for creating a sectional party or at least a sectional faction —the solid South. Except when his own presidential hopes were active and his own chances appeared to be good, he was inclined to turn away from the game of politics as it was customarily played—and still is.

In sum, the new interpreters of Calhoun have been careless in their reading of his philosophy and superficial in their description of current politics. They have attributed to him the very political principles and practices which he detested and for which he sought quite different alternatives. Without realizing it, they have misused the term "concurrent majority" so as to make it mean essentially what he himself meant by the term "numerical majority," that is, a combination of the majorities of many or even most *but not all* interests.

It might, or might not, be a good thing if the United States actually had institutions to give effect to the kind of "political pluralism" that the neo-Calhounites admire. It might be desirable, for instance, to set up a third house as a supplement to Congress, a third house in which economic, sectional, religious, racial, and other groups would be represented as such; and in which each of them could exercise a veto. Possibly this would work, and possibly it could be considered as a Calhounian solution—but only if certain passages are isolated from his works, unrestrained inferences are drawn from these passages, and the rest of his writings and his career itself are ignored.

On the whole, he seems to have taken a dualist, not a pluralist, view of politics. Though he mentioned the existence of various interests in society, he made no attempt to list and describe them, and certainly he never specified racial or religious minorities, or the working class, as deserving of the veto power. Generally he ignored the variety of possible groupings. When he got down to theorizing, he really thought about only two groups at a time, not several. On occasion he dealt with the duality of capital and labor. Most often he had in mind the twofold grouping of North against South, free states against slave states. These were, to him, the majority and the minority, and this was the minority he sought to protect—the minority of slaveholders.

It is farfetched to say that his "insights remain vital for any minority." This might be remotely true if his theory were abstracted enough, but the theory would have to be stretched to the point where it had only the most tenuous connection with what Calhoun actually thought and said. The assumption would have to be made that, somehow, the case for the onetime master has been, or at least can be, converted into a case for the onetime slave. This assumption has yet to be proved. Perhaps the National Association for the Advancement of Colored People ought to peruse Calhoun's works for means of protecting Negro rights. If the N.A.A.C.P. should do so, the news would be startling, and if the search were successful, the news would be amazing.

Surely the spirit of Calhoun is not to be found in the meetings of today's minority groups, of whatever creed or color. Nor is it to be discovered in all the political bargaining of the lobby, the congressional bloc, the executive department, or the smoke-filled room. We of the twentieth century must look elsewhere if we are to find the genuine ghost of the Great Nullifier.

THE CONTINUING RELEVANCE

Wherever a White Citizens' Council meets in Mississippi, or a similar group in another of the Southern states, *there* is to be sought, nowadays, the true spirit of Calhoun. It is to be sought in the activities of conservative—or reactionary—Southern whites. The way *they* use the lobby, the bloc, the party convention, and other political devices can be considered as essentially Calhounian.

These white Southerners now face a problem quite similar to the one that Calhoun faced more than a hundred years ago. They talk of maintaining white supremacy and he talked of protecting slavery. The problem remains that of defending, against external attack, institutions based upon a belief in human inequality.

One of Calhoun's proslavery arguments was this: that to turn the Negroes loose without giving them full civic rights (which he thought them by nature unfitted for) would only be to change the form of their bondage—they would cease to be the property of individual masters but would become the slaves of the community as a whole. As applied to the group servitude which Calhoun thus foresaw, abolition continues to be a live issue in the South. In the New Deal days, for example, the W.P.A. was an antislavery agency to the extent that it provided, at comparatively high pay, alternative employment for previously dependent "colored help." During the Second World War the manpower shortage and the Fair Employment Practices Commission brought additional job opportunities, and these also had an abolitionist effect. So did the wartime propaganda directed against racist notions and, as in the Four Freedoms slogan, in favor of human rights. Since the war, the emancipationist trend has been continued and accelerated by the civil-rights program of the Truman Administration, the diplomatic requirements of the Cold War, and the Supreme Court's reinterpretation of the Thirteenth and Fourteenth Amendments, especially in the historic case of *Brown* v. *Topeka* (1954), requiring desegregation of public schools.

In the face of the new abolitionism, Southern leaders of the present have responded in much the same way that Calhoun responded to the antislavery movement of his time. As has been seen, he resorted to the doctrine of state rights and to political devices, such as nullification, with which to implement the doctrine. He maintained that a "union" of Southerners would benefit the Union itself, that it was essential to the smooth working of the machinery of the federal Constitution. "The machine never works well when the South is divided," he said, "nor badly when it is united." Not only, then, did he call upon Southerners to unite; he also strove to win Northern sympathy and support for his united South. If such a combination had been attainable on his terms, he would have preferred an alliance of Northern and Southern conservatives. He withdrew temporarily from the party of Andrew Jackson, and on two occasions (1832 and 1836) when he disapproved both major parties and their presidential candidates, he advised that South Carolina cast her electoral votes for a third, irregular ticket. Finally he rejoined the Democratic party, but for reasons of expediency, not principle. He continued to hope that events ultimately would bring the conservatives of both sections into a single national party.

Recently, many Southern politicians have resorted to tactics that are reminiscent of Calhoun's. Within Congress, these politicians have formed blocs and, by means of them, have exercised a kind of concurrent veto at times, as in the Senate filibusters against civil-rights legislation in 1949 and subsequent years. Repeatedly, in presidential elections, the more extreme Southerners have threatened to withhold from the Democratic candidate the electoral votes of their states. In 1948 South Carolina and a few others actually did so, throwing their votes to the irregular, Dixiecratic candidate, J. Strom Thurmond (much as South Carolina had twice done more than a century earlier). In 1952, when Alabama's Senator Russell proposed to seek the Democratic nomination, the Southern Democrats were reminding their Northern partisans that, if the party should commit itself too strongly to civil rights, the Southerners might revolt again.

The Dixiecrats, legitimate heirs of Calhoun, relied in the 1940's, as he had done in the 1840's, on the hope that labor troubles in the North would bring Northern conservatives to the Southern cause.[57] This dream of a party realignment, one that would bring together the property interests of both sections within a single organization, has recurred from time to time in the minds of both Northerners and Southerners during the years since Calhoun's death.

For a quarter of a century the sectional conflict and the Civil War made impossible the realization of the dream. Then, in the Compromise of 1877, by which the Southerners agreed to the seating of Rutherford B. Hayes as President, despite his dubious electoral majority, the Hayes Republicans attempted to replace their Negro and carpetbagger allies with substantial white men, especially the old Whigs, in the South. This was, as C. Vann Woodward has termed it, a scheme of "reunion and reaction."[58] It had only a limited and temporary success.

At last, in 1952, exactly a hundred years after Daniel Webster had proposed a new party of Northern and Southern conservatives, a party of that kind seemed to be in the making, with Dwight D. Eisenhower as its chief. Two years later the Charlestonian Herbert Ravenel Sass contended that the American republic had already adapted itself to Calhounian principles but must adapt itself still further. "It is now in the process of adapting itself," Sass wrote, "and this further and far-reaching adaptation to Calhoun's blueprint reflects the revolution in political philosophy of which the Eisenhower victory of 1952 was a symptom. It is a counter-revolution against the national socialism which is the inevitable sequel of the concept of the republic as a single standardized equalitarian unit." [59] Without accepting all of Sass's implications, one can agree that the Eisenhower election, to the extent that it actually represented a conservative North-South reaction against current trends, exemplified the materialization, at least incipient, of Calhounian hopes.

During the presidency of Eisenhower and also that of John F. Kennedy, conservative Democrats from the South and conservative Republicans from the North have cooperated again and again in Congress. Still, in opposing the integration of schools and other public facilities, the Southern bloc has not, of itself, provided the sort of veto that Calhoun envisaged in nullification. Some of the Southerners have revived the idea of nullification itself, though they call it "interposition"—an alternative term that Calhoun also used. For instance, the *Richmond News Leader,* in 1955, devoted a special supplement to this theme. The editors called for "Interposition Now!" They reprinted Jefferson's and Madison's Kentucky and Virginia resolutions and, filling five columns, one of Calhoun's statements of "the right of interposition." The editors, asserting that the right still existed, called attention to his view of it as "the fundamental principle of our system, resting on facts historically as certain as our revolution itself, and deductions as simple and demonstrative [demonstrable] as that of any political or moral truth whatever." [60]

Several of the Southern states later passed interposition resolutions, though none of the states actually attempted to interpose against, or nullify, the Supreme Court's decision of 1954 or any of the federal measures intended to give effect to the decision.[61]

The die-hard defenders of segregation are thoroughly justified in thinking of themselves as successors and inheritors of Calhoun. It remains to be seen whether they can succeed any better than he did in making state rights a barrier to human rights.

Part 4

THE LITERATURE OF THE SUBJECT

This is a selective bibliography. It does not include quite all the items cited in the footnotes of the present work. It is, however, intended to direct the reader to the most significant discussions of Calhoun's career and thought. For additional references, the inquiring reader should consult the extensive bibliographies in the three-volume biography by Charles M. Wiltse, which is mentioned below. See also Harold S. Schultz, "A Century of Calhoun Biographies," *The South Atlantic Quarterly*, L (April, 1951), 248–54.

CALHOUN'S OWN WRITINGS

As yet, the only general collection of Calhoun's own writings is to be found in *The Works of John C. Calhoun*, ed. Richard K. Crallé (6 vols., Charleston, S.C.: Walker & James, and New York: D. Appleton & Co., 1851–56). Volume I contains the *Disquisition on Government* and the *Discourse on the Constitution and Government of the United States;* volumes II–IV, speeches; and volumes V–VI, reports and public letters. This collection is incomplete and, at certain points, not quite reliable. As therein reprinted, the earlier speeches were copied from reports in the *National Intelligencer,* a Washington newspaper, and some of the speeches were revised in the process. These *Works* may be supplemented by the *Correspondence of John C. Calhoun,* ed. J. F. Jameson (Vol. II, *Annual*

Report of the American Historical Association for the Year 1899, Washington, 1900), the largest published collection of Calhoun's personal and political letters. Both the *Works* and the *Correspondence* eventually will be supplanted by *The Papers of John C. Calhoun,* which is expected to run to fifteen volumes. The first volume, ed. Robert L. Meriwether (Columbia, S.C.: University of South Carolina Press, 1959), covers the years 1801–17. The papers as here presented are properly and carefully edited; they follow the original manuscripts or, where these are unavailable, the earliest or most reliable printed sources. The most noteworthy of the recent published selections from Calhoun's writings is *Calhoun: Basic Documents,* ed. John M. Anderson (State College, Pa.: Bald Eagle Press, 1952). This sampler begins with an 18-page introduction summarizing Calhoun's ideas on "political unity and sectionalism," "the development of social structure," "powers and principles," and "responsibility and freedom." Next comes the *Disquisition,* taken from the Crallé *Works,* and then follows a group of eleven speeches, all but one of them reproduced from the published records of congressional debates.

Among Calhoun's own writings should probably be listed the *Life of John C. Calhoun, Presenting a Condensed History of Political Events from 1811 to 1834* (New York: Harper & Bros., 1843). This flattering campaign document was published anonymously and, at the time, was commonly attributed to Calhoun's Virginia friend R. M. T. Hunter. In 1854 R. B. Rhett informed Richard K. Crallé that the book actually had been written by Calhoun himself, that Hunter only "inserted a page and a half, and became the putative author." As to the extent of Calhoun's authorship, his recent biographers differ. Charles M. Wiltse maintains that the book "is not in any legitimate sense of the

word an autobiography." Gerald M. Capers disagrees.
See Capers, as listed below, pp. 255–56.

BIOGRAPHIES

"There is no adequate Life of Calhoun," wrote William M. Meigs in the preface to his *The Life of John Caldwell Calhoun* (2 vols., New York: Neale Publishing Co., 1917). At the time Meigs wrote, Calhoun was indeed a neglected figure. The only earlier biographies worth noting were those by John S. Jenkins (1850), Herman Von Holst (1882), and Gaillard Hunt (1908). All these were brief, and each of them in one way or another was lacking in objectivity. For many years the work of Meigs, unimaginative but informative, remained the chief reliance for students of Calhoun.

The next book-length study to appear is imaginative but uninformative. This is Arthur Styron's *The Cast-Iron Man: John C. Calhoun and American Democracy* (New York: Longmans, Green & Co., 1935). The author, born in North Carolina, was an Episcopal clergyman. He has "a strong Catholic or High Episcopal bias," to quote the judgment of Harold S. Schultz. "Styron's aversion to Puritanism, which he identified with all the great economic and social changes in the Northern United States in the first half of the nineteenth century, seems to have moved him to write this biography."

At last Calhoun is given a full and scholarly treatment in the three-volume *John C. Calhoun* of Charles M. Wiltse. His first volume is subtitled *Nationalist, 1782–1828;* his second, *Nullifier, 1829–1839,* and his third, *Sectionalist, 1840–1850* (Indianapolis: Bobbs-Merrill, 1944, 1949, 1951). See the reviews by Richard N. Current in the *American Historical Review*, L (April, 1945), 550–51, and the *Mississippi Valley His-*

torical Review, XXXVI (December 1949), 513–14, and XXXVIII (March, 1952), 707–9. Wiltse's biography, on the whole an impressive accomplishment, is now the standard.

Two other recent biographies have merits of their own. Margaret L. Coit, *John C. Calhoun: American Portrait* (Boston: Houghton Mifflin, 1950), winner of a Pulitzer Prize, succeeds in making the so-called "cast-iron man" come alive as a flesh-and-blood human being. Miss Coit is less successful in dealing with his political career and constitutional philosophy. She follows Wiltse, Schlesinger, and other neo-Calhounites in viewing him as a "minority champion." Gerald M. Capers, *John C. Calhoun, Opportunist: A Reappraisal* (Gainesville, Fla.: University of Florida Press, 1960), though brief, is refreshingly critical and realistic. This book should be taken as an antidote to some of the more eulogistic passages in the Wiltse and Coit biographies.

SOME STUDIES OF POLITICAL THOUGHT

Among the older but still useful studies of aspects of Calhoun's thinking are William E. Dodd, *Statesmen of the Old South, or from Radicalism to Conservative Revolt* (New York: Macmillan Co., 1911), and Charles E. Merriam, "The Political Philosophy of John C. Calhoun," *Studies in Southern History and Politics, Inscribed to William Archibald Dunning . . . by His Former Pupils the Authors* (New York: Columbia University Press, 1914), pp. 317–38. Dodd traces changes in Southern thought through the careers of Thomas Jefferson, Jefferson Davis, and Calhoun. A professor of history at the University of Chicago, Dodd writes from the standpoint of contemporary progressivism. He sees Jefferson as something of a "populist," and Calhoun and Davis as representatives of "the interests."

Ralph Henry Gabriel, *The Course of American Democratic Thought: An Intellectual History Since 1815* (New York: Ronald Press Co., 1940), contains a chapter (pp. 103–10) entitled "A Footnote on John C. Calhoun," in which Gabriel makes this astonishing statement (p. 110): "Calhoun accepted the American democratic faith in all its doctrines." Such a statement can be sustained only by ignoring Calhoun's repudiation of the Jeffersonian belief that men are born with equal political rights and opportunities (surely an essential article of the American democratic faith!) and by defining that faith in some special, restrictive way. Gabriel defines it as a belief in the following: (1) fundamental law, (2) progress, and (3) liberty. It may be questioned whether Calhoun adhered to the American democratic faith, even if it is so defined, for he did not take quite the same view of fundamental law, progress, and liberty as did most of his contemporaries.

August O. Spain, *The Political Theory of John C. Calhoun* (New York: Twayne Publishers, 1951), is uncritical and incomplete but is nevertheless useful, especially in relating Calhoun's ideas to the thought of his contemporaries and predecessors. Louis Hartz reappraises the nullification doctrine in "South Carolina vs. the United States," *America in Crisis,* ed. Daniel Aaron (New York: Alfred A. Knopf, 1952), pp. 73–89. Margaret L. Coit, "Calhoun and the Downfall of States' Rights," *The Virginia Quarterly Review,* XXVIII (Spring, 1952), 191–208, contends that Calhoun, "by 1850, in practice, if not in theory, had repudiated the whole states'-rights doctrine" and had come to think only of "the South." Much more informed and perceptive in viewing the states'-rights argument is Arthur Bestor, "State Sovereignty and Slavery: A Reinterpretation of Proslavery Constitutional Doctrine, 1846–1860," *Journal of the Illinois State Historical Society,* LIV (Summer, 1961), 1–64. Bestor does not deal specifically with Calhoun but treats, in a new light, the Southern viewpoint which, in some of its aspects, Calhoun shared.

VIEWS OF THE NEO-CALHOUNITES

Vernon L. Parrington seems to have originated the notion that Calhoun's theory of the concurrent majority has some special relevance for our times. In *The Romantic Revolution in America, Main Currents in American Thought,* Vol. II, New York, 1926, Parrington suggests (p. 77) that "Calhoun was face to face with a revolutionary conception—the conception of proportional economic representation." Charles M. Wiltse elaborates upon the idea in "Calhoun and the Modern State," *The Virginia Quarterly Review,* XIII (Summer, 1937), 396–408, and in "Calhoun's Democracy," *The Journal of Politics,* III (May, 1941), 210–23. Herbert Agar, *Pursuit of Happiness: The Story of American Democracy* (Boston: Houghton Mifflin Co., 1938), appears indebted to Wiltse's essay of the previous year; he says: "We can take lessons from Calhoun without becoming candidates for the Liberty League." Hamilton Basso, *Mainstream* (New York: Reynal & Hitchcock, 1943), also holds that the "concept of proportional representation" is implicit in Calhoun's idea of the concurrent majority, but he concedes: "The validity of Calhoun's view is still a matter of debate. . . ."

In his treatment of Calhoun, Arthur M. Schlesinger, Jr., *The Age of Jackson* (Boston: Little, Brown & Co., 1945), agrees with the neo-Calhounites. Schlesinger misconstrues Calhoun at several points, but worst of all in explaining Calhoun's decision to abandon his Whig allies and combine with the Democrats in 1837. Schlesinger says:

The Southern dilemma was this: which was the greater menace to the plantation system—radical democracy or finance capital? Should the ruling class of the South ally itself to the upper class of the North, and thus to broad construction, capitalism and conservatism, or to the lower classes of the North, and thus to State rights, agrarianism and reform? Should the South join the Whigs in their fight against radicalism, or should it join the Democrats in their fight against business rule? (p. 244)

In the end Calhoun could not but see the struggle in Jeffersonian terms, between landed capital and business capital—not, as the Southern Whigs saw it, in Federalist terms, between property, whether in land or business, and the propertyless. His decision showed how profoundly he inherited the Jeffersonian tradition. (p. 246)

Indeed, his fear of radical democracy, with its equalitarian and majoritarian tendencies, remained second only to his fear of capitalism itself. (p. 247)

Now, there is not a shred of evidence in Calhoun's writings to support that interpretation. The evidence, as I have tried to show in the preceding pages, leads to quite a different conclusion. To the end of his life Calhoun continued to believe that the property owners of the North were the natural allies of the property owners of the South. In politics, it is true, he aligned himself after 1837 with the party of the Northern "radicals," but he did so as a second choice, and for reasons of expediency, not principle.

Peter F. Drucker, "A Key to American Politics: Calhoun's Pluralism," *The Review of Politics*, X (October, 1948), 412–26, develops most fully the neo-Calhounite misconceptions. John Fischer, "Unwritten Rules of American Politics," *Harper's Magazine*, CXCVII (November, 1948), 27–36, merely quotes and paraphrases the Drucker essay, published the preceding month. "The Negative Power," *Time,* May 19, 1952, pp. 29–32, further popularizes the Wiltse-Drucker-Fischer view and applies it to current events. Herbert Ravenel Sass, "They Don't Tell the Truth about the South," *The Saturday Evening Post,* January 9, 1954, pp. 25, 67–68, makes use of the idea in a denunciation of Northerners and the North.

DISSENTING VIEWS

Richard N. Current, "John C. Calhoun, Philosopher of Reaction," *Antioch Review,* III (Summer, 1943), 223–34, calls attention to the place of the class-struggle concept in the thinking of Calhoun. I began this study in 1936, while a student of Professor William B. Hesseltine at the University of Wisconsin. I am much indebted to Professor Hesseltine for suggesting the topic as one worth exploring. In *Daniel Webster and the Rise of National Conservatism* (Boston: Little, Brown & Co., 1955), I compare Webster's conservative philosophy with Calhoun's reactionary philosophy and offer a brief critique of the neo-Calhounite view.

Richard Hofstadter carries further the conception of Calhoun as, in his words, "the Marx of the Master Class," in a chapter (pp. 67–91) of *The American Political Tradition and the Men Who Made It* (New York: Alfred A. Knopf, 1948). Hofstadter discusses, with aptness and insight, the relation of Calhounism to current events in his essay "From Calhoun to the Dixiecrats," *Social Research,* XVI (June, 1949), 136–50.

NOTES

Part 1.

1. Margaret L. Coit, *John C. Calhoun: American Portrait* (Boston: Houghton Mifflin Co., 1950), p. 531.

2. The fullest account of Calhoun's early years is to be found in Charles M. Wiltse, *John C. Calhoun: Nationalist, 1782–1828* (Indianapolis: Bobbs-Merrill, 1944), pp. 11–52. But see also Gerald M. Capers, *John C. Calhoun, Opportunist: A Reappraisal* (Gainesville, Fla.: University of Florida Press, 1960), pp. 1–24. For Calhoun's career as a whole, I have relied on both Wiltse's three-volume and Capers' one-volume biography.

3. Quoted in Capers, *op. cit.*, p. 31. See also *The Papers of John C. Calhoun*, ed. Robert L. Meriwether (Columbia, S.C.: University of South Carolina Press, 1959), I, 75–85.

4. Speech of February 4, 1817, *Papers . . .* , I, 401.

5. *Ibid.*, 403. In this quotation, I have changed the first sentence from the third to the first person, from indirect to direct discourse.

6. *The Works of John C. Calhoun*, ed. Richard K. Crallé (6 vols.; Charleston, S.C.: Walker & James, and New York: D. Appleton & Co., 1851–56), VI, 1–59. Hereafter cited as *Works*.

7. Wiltse, *John C. Calhoun: Nullifier, 1829–1839* (Indianapolis: Bobbs-Merrill, 1949), pp. 70–71.

8. *Works*, VI, 172.

9. Richard N. Current, *Daniel Webster and the Rise of National Conservatism* (Boston: Little, Brown & Co., 1955), p. 67.

10. Calhoun to Christopher Van Deventer, March 24, 1833, *Correspondence of John C. Calhoun*, ed. J. F. Jameson (Vol. II, *Annual Report of the American Historical As-*

sociation for the Year 1899, Washington, 1900), p. 324. Hereafter cited as *Correspondence*.

11. William B. Hesseltine, "Some New Aspects of the Proslavery Argument," *Journal of Negro History*, XXI (January, 1936), 1–15.

12. Calhoun to Armistead Burt, Sept. 1, 1831, *Correspondence*, p. 302.

13. *Works*, II, 631; III, 180.

14. *Ibid.*, 632–33.

15. See Richard N. Current, "John C. Calhoun, Philosopher of Reaction," *Antioch Review*, III (Summer, 1943), 223–34.

16. *Works*, III, 186.

17. Quoted in Capers, *op. cit.*, p. 202.

18. Calhoun to James H. Hammond, Sept. 24, 1841, *Correspondence*, p. 493.

19. Capers, *op. cit.*, pp. 255–56.

20. *Works*, V, 333–39.

21. *Ibid.*, IV, 308.

22. Calhoun to Mrs. T. G. Clemson, Dec. 27, 1846, *Correspondence*, p. 716.

23. *Works*, IV, 348.

24. Capers, *op. cit.*, p. 224.

25. Quoted in *ibid.*, p. 239.

26. Speech on Clay's proposed compromise, March 4, 1850, *Works*, IV, 573.

27. Current, *Daniel Webster . . .* , pp. 166–67.

28. Capers, *op. cit.*, p. 254.

Part 2.

1. Quoted in Richard N. Current, T. Harry Williams, and Frank Freidel, *American History: A Survey* (New York: Alfred A. Knopf, 1961), p. 75.

2. For Madison's view of the Constitution, see Edward M. Burns, *James Madison, Philosopher of the Constitution* (New Brunswick, N.J.: Rutgers University Press, 1938), pp. 91–103.

3. See Richard N. Current, *Daniel Webster and the Rise of National Conservatism* (Boston: Little, Brown & Co., 1955), p. 12.

4. *Ibid.*, p. 17.

5. On the background of the state-rights doctrine, see August O. Spain, *The Political Theory of John C. Calhoun* (New York: Twayne Publishers, 1951), pp. 45–68.

6. See *ibid.*, pp. 33–37, and Charles M. Wiltse, *John C. Calhoun: Sectionalist, 1840–1850* (Indianapolis: Bobbs-Merrill, 1951), pp. 420–23.

7. *The Works of John C. Calhoun*, ed. Richard K. Crallé (6 vols.; Charleston, S.C.: Walker & James, and New York: D. Appleton & Co., 1851–56), I, 1–7, 56–57. Hereafter cited as *Works*.

8. *Ibid.*, IV, 507–9.

9. *Disquisition on Government*, in *ibid.*, I, 55, 59.

10. *Ibid.*, 7, 13–24.

11. *Ibid.*, 24–37.

12. *Ibid.*, 37–38, 48–49, 64–73.

13. *Discourse on the Constitution and Government of the United States*, in *ibid.*, 399–405.

14. *Disquisition . . .* , in *ibid.*, 91–106.

15. Calhoun to Thomas G. Clemson, March 22, 1848, and May 26, 1848; to J. E. Calhoun, April 15, 1848; and to Mrs. T. G. Clemson, June 23, 1848, *Correspondence of John C. Calhoun*, ed. J. F. Jameson (Vol. II, *Annual Report of the American Historical Association for the Year 1899*, Washington, 1900), pp. 746–47, 749–50, 756–58. Hereafter cited as *Correspondence*.

16. *Disquisition . . .* , *op. cit.*, I, 75–77; *Discourse . . .* , in *ibid.*, 174–87, 228–39.

17. *Ibid.*, 393–95.

18. Spain, *op. cit.*, pp. 164–72.

19. *Discourse . . .* , I, 114–26, 146, 189–92.

20. *Ibid.*, 111.

21. *Ibid.*, 119–23, 125–26.

22. Reply to Webster, February 26, 1833, *ibid.*, II, 282. See also *ibid.*, I, 113–18, and IV, 356.

23. Address on the Relation of the States and the Federal Government, 1831, *ibid.*, VI, 73.

24. *Discourse* . . . , in *ibid.*, I, 295–96.

25. *Ibid.*, 172–73.

26. Lincoln, for example, composed in 1852 a set of resolutions the first of which maintained "That it is the right of any people, sufficiently numerous for national independence, to throw off, to revolutionize, their existing form of government, and to establish such other in its stead as they may choose." *The Collected Works of Abraham Lincoln*, ed. Roy P. Basler (9 vols. and index; New Brunswick, N.J.: Rutgers University Press, 1953–55), II, 115.

27. *Works*, I, 300–301.

28. *Ibid.*, IV, 528; VI, 293.

29. *Ibid.*, VI, 309–11.

30. *Ibid.*, 307–9.

31. *Ibid.*, I, 388–89.

32. *Ibid.*, V, 334, 336.

33. *Ibid.*, IV, 479–80,, 496–98. Regarding the mails, in a speech of April 12, 1836, Calhoun asked: "Will any rational being say that the laws of eleven States of this Union, which are necessary to their peace, security, and very existence, ought to yield to the laws of the General Government regulating the post-office, which at the best is a mere accommodation and convenience—and this when the Government was formed *by the States* mainly with a view to secure more perfectly their peace and safety?" *Ibid.*, II, 527.

34. The implications of Calhoun's class-struggle theory were first developed in Richard N. Current, "John C. Calhoun, Philosopher of Reaction," *Antioch Review*, II (Summer, 1943), 223–34.

35. Report on Abolition Petitions, February 4, 1836, *Works*, V, 207–8.

36. Speech on Reception of Abolition Petitions, February 6, 1837, *ibid.*, II, 631–32.

37. *Ibid.*, IV, 196.

38. Anonymous memorandum of a conversation with Calhoun, December 4, 1831, *Correspondence*, p. 305.

39. "South Carolina Exposition," *Works*, VI, 25–26.

40. Speech of February 6, 1837, *ibid.*, II, 631.

41. Remarks on State Rights Resolutions, January 12, 1838, *ibid.*, III, 180.

42. Remarks on the Territories, February 20, 1847, *ibid.*, IV, 360–61; *Disquisition* . . . , in *ibid.*, I, 46.

43. Calhoun to Mrs. T. G. Clemson, November 21, 1846; April 28, 1848, *Correspondence*, pp. 712, 752–53.

44. *Works*, I, 86–91.

45. *Correspondence*, pp. 750–58; *Works*, IV, 450–52.

46. *Works*, V, 207–8.

47. *Ibid.*, II, 631–32; III, 180.

48. *Ibid.*, IV, 360–61.

49. *Ibid.*, 532–33.

50. *Ibid.*, III, 477–86.

51. *Ibid.*, III, 459; IV, 183, 385, 521.

52. *Ibid.*, III, 431, 436–37; IV, 115; Calhoun to Abbott Lawrence, May 13, 1845, *Correspondence*, pp. 655–56.

53. *Works*, I, 46–49; VI, 233.

54. *Ibid.*, III, 195.

55. *Ibid.*, VI, 25–26.

56. *Ibid.*, IV, 25.

57. *Ibid.*, 413–14.

58. Calhoun to S. L. Gouverneur, August 18, 1831, *Correspondence*, p. 300.

59. Calhoun to J. E. Calhoun, February 4, 1834, *ibid.*, p. 331.

60. Calhoun to Duff Green, August 30, 1835, *ibid.*, pp. 344–45.

61. Calhoun to A. P. Calhoun, April 16, 1848, *ibid.*, p. 750.

Part 3.

1. William M. Meigs, *The Life of John Caldwell Calhoun* (2 vols.; New York: Neale Publishing Co., 1917), II, 107.

2. *The Works of John C. Calhoun*, ed. Richard K. Crallé (6 vols.; Charleston, S.C.: Walker & James, and New York: D. Appleton & Co., 1851–56), II, 232–33.

3. Harriet Martineau, *Retrospect of Western Travel* (2 vols.; London: Saunders and Otley, 1838), I, 147–48.

4. Calhoun skirted the question when he attacked the idea of "popular sovereignty" in the territories, June 27, 1848. *Works* . . . , IV, 498–99. He also evaded the question in discussing the bill for the admission of Michigan as a state, January 2, 1837. *Ibid.*, II, 586–96.

5. Richard N. Current, *Daniel Webster and the Rise of National Conservatism* (Boston: Little, Brown & Co., 1955), pp. 67–68.

6. Charles M. Wiltse, *John C. Calhoun: Nullifier, 1829–1839* (Indianapolis: Bobbs-Merrill, 1949), p. 88.

7. Current, *op. cit.*, pp. 35–36, 38.

8. Thomas Hamilton, *Men and Manners in America* (Philadelphia: Carey, Lea & Blanchard, 1833), pp. 161–64.

9. Current, *op. cit.*, pp. 145–46.

10. *Ibid.*, pp. 147–50.

11. *The Works of Daniel Webster* (6 vols., Boston: Little, Brown & Co., 1853), II, 405.

12. Current, *Old Thad Stevens: A Story of Ambition* (Madison, Wis.: University of Wisconsin Press, 1942), pp. 41–42, 45–46.

13. ———, *Daniel Webster* . . . , pp. 177–78.

14. *The Collected Works of Abraham Lincoln,* ed. Roy P. Basler (9 vols.; New Brunswick, N.J.: Rutgers University Press, 1953–55), IV, 438; Jefferson Davis, *The Rise and Fall of the Confederate Government* (2 vols.; New York: D. Appleton & Co., 1881), I, 232.

15. This is the thesis of William E. Dodd, *Statesmen of the Old South, or from Radicalism to Conservative Revolt* (New York: Macmillan Co., 1911), though Dodd deals only with Jefferson, Calhoun, and Davis. See especially pp. 232–35.

16. Glover Moore, *The Missouri Controversy, 1819– 1821* (Lexington, Ky.: University of Kentucky Press, 1953), pp. 254–55.

17. Henry Adams, *John Randolph* (Boston: Houghton Mifflin Co., 1882), pp. 268, 270, 286, 288–89, 301.

18. Calhoun, *Works . . . ,* III, 185.

19. Adams, *op. cit.,* p. 270.

20. Calhoun, *Works . . . ,* IV, 490–94.

21. Avery Craven, *The Coming of the Civil War* (Chicago: University of Chicago Press, 1957), pp. 257–58.

22. Hudson Strode, *Jefferson Davis, Confederate President* (New York: Harcourt, Brace & World, 1959), p. 491.

23. U. B. Phillips, *The Course of the South to Secession* (New York: D. Appleton-Century Co., 1939), p. 134.

24. Craven, *op. cit.,* p. 258.

25. Wiltse, *John C. Calhoun: Sectionalist, 1840–1850* (Indianapolis: Bobbs-Merrill, 1951), p. 479.

26. See Arthur Bestor, "State Sovereignty and Slavery: A reinterpretation of Proslavery Constitutional Doctrine, 1846–1860," *Journal of the Illinois State Historical Society,* LIV (1961), 15, 24, 31, 51–56.

27. Dodd, *op. cit.,* pp. 225–27.

28. Quoted in Alexander H. Stephens, *A Constitutional View of the Late War Between the States* (2 vols.; New York; 1868–70), I, 416–17.

29. Quoted in Phillip Van Doren Stern, *Prologue to Sumter* (Bloomington, Ind.: Indiana University Press, 1961), pp. 170–71.

30. Quoted in *Northern Editorials on Secession,* ed. Howard C. Perkins (2 vols.; New York: Appleton-Century-Crofts, 1942), I, 216. For similar quotations from other Northern papers, see *ibid.,* I, 168–69, 180; II, 823.

31. Stephens, *op. cit.,* I, 341.

32. *Ibid.,* I, 189.

33. Dodd, *op. cit.,* p. 166.

34. Meigs, *op. cit.,* II, 466–67n.

35. H. Von Holst, *John C. Calhoun* (Boston: Houghton Mifflin Co., 1882), pp. 3–4.

36. Dodd, *op. cit.,* p. 91.

37. Written by Charles M. Wiltse (3 vols., Indianapolis, Bobbs-Merrill 1944–51); Margaret L. Coit (Boston, Houghton-Mifflin 1950); and Gerald M. Capers (Gainesville, Fla., 1960).

38. Written by August O. Spain (New York, 1951).

39. *The New York Times,* April 19, 1953, sec. 1, p. 49, col. 1. The first volume of the *Papers of John C. Calhoun,* 1801–1817, was published by the University of South Carolina Press for the South Carolina Society in 1959.

40. John Fischer, "Unwritten Rules of American Politics," *Harper's Magazine,* CXCVII (November, 1948), 27–36.

41. "The Negative Power," *Time,* May 19, 1952, pp. 29–32.

42. Herbert Ravenel Sass, "They Don't Tell the Truth about the South," *Saturday Evening Post,* January 9, 1954, pp. 25, 67–68.

43. Paul H. Douglas, Review of *The American President* by Sidney Hyman, *The New York Times Book Review,* February 14, 1954, p. 6.

44. Peter F. Drucker, "A Key to American Politics: Calhoun's Pluralism," *The Review of Politics,* X (October, 1948), 412–26. The article by Fischer in *Harper's,* cited above, was based closely upon Drucker's essay.

45. Charles M. Wiltse, "Calhoun and the Modern State," *The Virginia Quarterly Review,* XIII (Summer, 1937), 396–408. For Parrington's earlier view, see his *The Ro-*

mantic Revolution in America (Vol. II, *Main Currents in American Thought*, New York, 1926), pp. 69–82.

46. Margaret L. Coit, *John C. Calhoun: American Portrait* (Boston: Houghton Mifflin Co., 1950), p. 518. Miss Coit entitled her concluding chapter "Minority Champion."

47. Arthur M. Schlesinger, Jr., *The Age of Jackson* (Boston: Little, Brown & Co., 1945), p. 405.

48. Russell Kirk, *The Conservative Mind* (Chicago: H. Regnery Co., 1953), pp. 194, 208–9.

49. Charles M. Wiltse, "Calhoun's Democracy," *The Journal of Politics*, III (May, 1941), 210–23. The quotation is from pp. 219–20.

50. Fischer, "Unwritten Rules . . . ," p. 33.

51. *Ibid.*

52. Drucker, "Key to American Politics . . . ," p. 415.

53. Calhoun, *Works* . . . , 1, 16.

54. Quoted in Charles E. Merriam, "The Political Philosophy of John C. Calhoun," *Studies in Southern History and Politics, Inscribed to William Archibald Dunning . . . by His Former Pupils the Authors* (New York: Columbia University Press, 1914), pp. 322–23.

55. Calhoun, *Works* . . . , IV, 393–94.

56. *Niles National Register*, LXXII (May 8, 1847), 148.

57. See Richard Hofstadter, "From Calhoun to the Dixiecrats," *Social Research*, XVI (June, 1949), 135–50. Hofstadter cites (p. 149) a book, *Whither Solid South?* (New Orleans, 1947), written by an Alabama lawyer and Dixiecrat named Collins, who "rests his hope for northern allies on a split, now actually far more decisive than it was in Calhoun's day, between conservatives and radicals in the North."

58. C. Vann Woodward, *Reunion and Reaction: The Compromise of 1877 and the End of Reconstruction* (Boston: Little, Brown & Co., 1951).

59. *The Saturday Evening Post*, January 9, 1954, p. 68.

60. *Richmond News Leader*, November 21, 1955. Among the many other references to interposition or nullification in connection with Southern resistance to integra-

tion, may be mentioned those in *The New York Times,* February 19, 1956, and the *Greensboro* (N.C.) *Daily News,* June 14, 1956.

61. See, for example, *The New York Times,* September 22, 1957, sec. 4, p. 1, col. 4. The Georgia Senate, February 8, 1957, adopted a bootless resolution declaring the Fourteenth and Fifteenth Amendments to the United States Constitution null and void. AP dispatch in the *Chicago Tribune,* February 9, 1957, sec. 1, p. 11, col. 1.

INDEX

Ableman v. Booth (1859), 133

Abolitionism, 19-20, 21-23, 27

Adams, Henry, 129, 130

Adams, John, 142

Adams, John Quincy, 9-10, 12

Agar, Herbert, 160

Age of Jackson, The (Schlesinger), 160-61

Alien and Sedition Acts (1798), 40

American Political Tradition and the Men Who Made It (Hofstadter), 162

Annual Report of the American Historical Association for the Year 1899, 155-156

Aristotle, 44

Basso, Hamilton, 160

Bestor, Arthur, 159-160

Blackstone, William 60, 112

Blair, Francis P., 131

Bodin, Jean, 60, 112

Brown, A. C., 133

Brown v. Topeka (1954), 149

Buchanan, James, 133

Burke, Edmund, 44

Burnaby, Andrew, 38

Calhoun: Basic Documents (Anderson), 156

Calhoun, Floride (daughter) *see* Calhoun, John C. (Mrs.)

Calhoun, Floride (mother), 5-6, 14

Calhoun, John C.
  background, 3-4
  biographies, 157-158
  class struggle and, 86-102, 105
  concurrent majority and, 49-60, 103
  conservatism and, 119, 122, 123-129
  constitutions, 103, 104
  death of, 33
  dual presidency, 105
  education, 4-5
  influence of, 107-112
  liberty, 45-48, 102-103
  literature concerning, 155-162
  logic and, 112-119
  marriage, 6
  nationalism and, 6-13
  neo–Calhounism, 136-146, 160-162
  nullification and, 13-19, 69-76, 103
  secession, 103-104
  sectionalism and, 19-34

slavery and, 19-34, 76-86, 104-105, 134

sovereignty, 104

state–rights doctrine and, 42-49, 76-86

theory of government, 37-105

writings, 154-157

Calhoun, John C. (Mrs.), 5-6, 14

Calhoun, Patrick, 4

California, 29, 31

Capers, Gerald M., 157, 158

Cast–Iron Man, John C. Calhoun and American Democracy, The (Styron), 157

Cherokee Indians, 16

Class struggle, 86, 105
exploitation, 87-91
northern interests and, 97-102
slavery and, 93-97
transitional period, 92-93

Clay, Henry, 6, 7, 9, 10, 17, 21, 25, 26, 31, 99, 112, 122, 134

Clayton, John M., 109

Coit, Margaret L., 142

Columbia Guardian (newspaper), 134

Commentaries (Blackstone), 60

Compromise of 1877, 150

Compromise Tariff, 18

Concurrent majority, 103
constitutional government and, 40-50, 51
examples of, 55-59

government by, 55
"mutual negative," 52
suffrage and, 50-51
unanimous consent, 53-54
U.S. Constitution and, 59-60

Conservatism, 119-127

Constitutional View of the War between the States, A (Stephens), 136

Constitutions, 49-52, 103, 104

Cooper, Thomas, 43

Correspondence of John C. Calhoun (Jameson), 155-156

Course of American Democratic Thought: An Intellectual History Since 1815 (Gabriel), 159

Crallé, Richard K., 155, 156

Crawford, William C., 9, 42

Creek Indians, 16

Current, Richard N., 157, 162

Daniel Webster and the Rise of National Conservatism (Current), 162

Davis, Jefferson, 127-128, 131, 133, 134, 135, 136

Democrat party, 25-26, 125, 143, 145

Discourse on the Constitution and Government of the United States (Calhoun), 37

Disquisition on Government, A (Calhoun), 37, 44, 101, 137, 139, 156

Dixiecrats, 150

Dodd, William E., 133, 137, 158
Douglas, Paul H., 139-140
Douglas, Stephen A., 30, 133
Dred Scott case (1858), 132
Drucker, Peter F., 140-141, 161
Dwight, Timothy, 5

Eaton, Peggy O'Neal Timberlake, 14
Eisenhower, Dwight D., 150-151
Engels, Friedrich, 87, 91
Equality, 46-48
Essex Junto, 41

Fair Employment Practices Commission, 140
Federalist party, 39-40, 41
Fischer, John, 161
Force Bill, 16, 18
Fort Hill Letter, 15
France, 58
Franklin, Benjamin, 37
Free–Soil Democrats, 31

Gabriel, Ralph Henry, 159
Garrison, William Lloyd, 19
Georgia, 135
Germany, 58
Government, theory of
    class struggle, 86-102, 105
  concurrent majority principle, 49-60, 103
  constitution, 49-53, 103-104
  dual presidency, 59-60, 105

liberty, 102-103
man and, 43-49, 102
nullification, 60-76, 103
secession, 103-104
slavery, 76-86, 104-105
sovereignty, 104
states-rights doctrine, 37-49, 76-86
Great Britain, 26, 28, 56, 57-58, 97

Hamilton, Alexander, 38, 39, 122
Hamilton, Thomas, 120
Harper's Magazine, 137, 138
Harrison, William Henry, 25
Hartford Convention (1814-15), 42
Hartz, Louis, 159
Hayes, Rutherford B., 150
Hayne, Robert Y., 15, 16
Hesseltine, William B., 162
Hobbes, Thomas, 43, 44, 60
Hofstadter, Richard, 162
Holst, Herman Von, 157
Human nature, 43-49, 102
Hunt, Gaillard, 157
Hunter, R. M. T., 156

Iroquois Indians, 55

Jackson, Andrew, 8, 9, 12, 14, 15, 16, 18, 21, 23, 120-121, 124, 134, 135
Jacksonian radicals, 121-122
Jefferson, Thomas, 5, 9, 11, 39, 40, 41, 42, 43, 64, 71, 128, 129, 130, 131, 133
Jeffersonian democracy, 128.

Jenkins, John S., 157
John C. Calhoun: American Portrait (Coit), 158
John C. Calhoun, Opportunits: A Reappraisal (Capers), 158
John C. Calhoun (Wiltse), 157-158

Kennedy, John F., 151
Kentucky resolution (1798-99), 40, 71, 128
Kirk, Russell, 142

Liberator (newspaper), 19
Liberty, 45-48
Liberty party, 31
Life of John Caldwell Calhoun, The (Meigs), 157
Life of John C. Calhoun, Presenting a Condensed History of Political Events from 1811 to 1834 (Calhoun), 156
Lincoln, Abraham, 74, 127
Livingston, Edward, 134
Locke, John, 43, 44, 74, 87
Loco Focos, 120, 125
Louisiana, 41, 115

Madison, James, 7, 38, 39, 40, 41, 43, 61, 71, 118
Mainstream (Basso), 160
Man, relation to society, 43-49, 102
Marshall, John, 16, 62
Martineau, Harriet, 111
Marx, Karl, 87, 88, 90, 91, 101
Meigs, William M., 157

Meriwether, Robert L., 156
Merriam, Charles E., 158
Mexican War, 29
Mexico, 28
Missouri Compromise, 129-130
Monroe, James, 8

Nat Turner insurrection, 19
National Association for the Advancement of Colored People (N.A.A.C.P.) 147
National Intelligencer (newspaper), 155
Nationalism, 6-13
Neo–Calhounism, 136-147, 160-162
New York Evening Post (newspaper), 27
New York Times (newspaper, 139
North Carolina, 135
Northwest Ordinance (1787), 82
Nullification, 13-19, 103
    amendments and, 70-73
    secession and, 73-76
    state sovereignty and, 60-69

Oregon, 28, 29-30

Papers of John C. Calhoun, The (Meriwether), 156
Parrington, V. L., 141, 160
Patricians, 56
Perry, Benjamin F., 132
Philadelphia Press (newspaper), 134

Plebeians, 56

Poland, 55, 117

Political Theory of John C. Calhoun, The (Spain), 159

Polk, James K., 26, 27, 28

Presidency, dual 105

Prigg v. the Commonwealth of Pennsylvania (1842), 75

Progress, 46-47

Pursuit of Happiness: The Story of American Democracy (Agar), 160

Quids, 42

Randolph, John, 12, 42, 43, 128, 129, 130, 131

Reeve, Tapping, 5

Republican party, 39-40, 41, 142-143

Rhett, Robert Barnwell, 131-132, 133, 156

Richmond News Leader (newspaper) 150

Rise and Fall of the Confederate Government, The (Davis), 136

Roane, Spencer, 42, 43, 61

Romantic Revolution in America. Main Currents in American Thought (Parrington), 160

Rome (ancient), 56-57

Roosevelt, Franklin D., 143

Russell, Richard, 138

Sass, Herbert Ravenel, 138-139, 151, 162

Saturday Evening Post, The (Magazine), 137, 139

Schlesinger, Arthur M. (Jr.), 142, 160-161

Schultz, Harold S., 155, 157

Secession, 73-76, 103-104

Sectionalism, 19-34

Security, 45

Sedition Act (1798), 40

Seward, William H., 31

Slavery, 19-34, 104-105

    constitutional compact and, 81

    state powers and, 76-86

    trust powers and, 83-84

South Carolina, 55-56

"South Carolina Exposition" (Calhoun), 13, 20, 99

South Carolina Unionists, 132

Southern Confederacy, 131

Sovereignty, state, 60-69, 104

Spain, August O., 159

Stanley, Lord, 95-96

Statesmen of the Old South, or from Radicalism to Conservative Revolt (Dodd), 158

States–rights doctrine, 37-49, 76-86

    precedents, 37-43

Stephens, Alexander H., 128, 135-136

Stevens, Thaddeus, 126

Styron, Arthur, 157

Taft–Hartly Act (1947), 142-143

Taney, Roger B., 132

Tariffs

    1816, 11

1828, 11-12
1832, 15
Taylor, John, 42, 43
Taylor, Zachary, 30-31
Texas, annexation, 26-27, 29
Thurmond, J. Strom, 150
Time (magazine), 137, 138
Treaty of Guadalupe Hidalgo, 29
Tucker, St. George, 42, 43, 61
Tyler, John, 24, 26

Underground Railway, 32
University of Virginia, 129

Value, labor theory of, 44
Van Buren, Martin, 14, 26, 31
Verplank Bill, 17
Virginia resolution (1798), 40, 71

Waddell, Moses, 5
Walker, Robert J., 121
Washington, George, 39
Webster–Calhoun debate, 17
Webster Daniel, 6, 11, 12, 17, 21, 31, 33, 41, 62, 74, 112, 115, 119-120, 122, 123-124, 125, 126-127, 134, 150
Whig party, 21-22, 25, 30, 31, 124
Wilmot, David, 29
Wilmot Proviso, 29
Wiltse, Charles M., 141, 142, 155, 156, 157-158, 160
Wisconsin, 133
Woodward, C. Vann, 150
Woolens Bill, 11
Works of John C. Calhoun, The (Crallé), 155, 156